THREATS OF INTERVENTION

THREATS OF INTERVENTION

▼

U.S.-Mexican Relations, 1917-1923

Drew Philip Halévy

Writers Club Press

San Jose New York Lincoln Shanghai

Threats of Intervention
U.S.-Mexican Relations, 1917-1923

Writers Club Press
an imprint of iUniverse.com, Inc.

For information address:
iUniverse.com, Inc.
5220 S 16th, Ste. 200
Lincoln, NE 68512
www.iuniverse.com

ISBN: 0-595-16433-1

Printed in the United States of America

This is dedicated to Dianna for putting up with me going to school for so long and to Max for being such a cute kid.

"Poor Mexico, so far from God, so close to the United States." Porfirio Diaz

CONTENTS

▼

FOREWORD

▼

This work started life as a master's thesis in the History Department at the University of Arkansas. I had entered the University of Arkansas in 1994 as a PhD. candidate, after doing independent study for two years under Dr. Stephen Strausberg, in the field of Latin America. After Dr. Strausberg passed away, I lost some of my enthusiasm for working on PhD, and I decided to switch to an MA in history. By 1996, I had started working in the computer field, and quite simply, I had lost my motivation to finish the MA, as I had more opportunities, and more challenges, in the computer field.

I tried to work on a thesis part-time under Dr. Randall Woods, but, as he rightly stated, I need to devote my efforts to the thesis full time or make some tough choices. I was resentful at the time, but in hindsight, I can see that Dr. Woods was giving me good advice, and the he had my best interests in mind. I decided to put the thesis aside and devote myself full time to the computer field.

It is now 5 years later, and it is a decision that I do not regret. However, I have held onto the thesis, and I have always wanted to present it in some manner. I had considered turning the thesis into a web page, but never got around to doing it. The thesis sat in a drawer, forgotten and unread.

While web surfing one day, I came across the IUniverse page, and I found the concept intriguing. After some investigation, I decided to go forward with publishing my thesis. I doubt that I will sell very many copies of my thesis, but it will still be neat to have it in print. While not the greatest work ever published, I think that this work is a good foundation for a later, larger work. Perhaps one day I will be doing book signings, but for now I will be happy with a few published copies and someone, anyone, buying my book.

PREFACE

▼

When I tell people that I am studying the diplomatic relations between the United States and Mexico, the first question that I am always asked is why Mexico. While there is no simple answer, the most concise response that I have found is that I find Mexico (and to a much lesser extent, Canada) fascinating. All three countries occupy the same continent and share undefended borders. Yet each is unique, politically, socially and culturally. North America and Mexico were settled within 150 years of one another by European powers. Mexico was different, to be sure, since a dynastic empire was already ruling it. Mexico was born of the collision between two distinct cultures, while in North America, the birth was more of an installation of a society into an area viewed as empty by those newly arrived. The two societies that evolved did so under two very different religions. While the point can be over emphasized, Protestant English America and Catholic New Spain lived under two very different socio-religious worldviews.

At first, it seemed that Mexico was the one with the brightest future. Gold and silver were being mined at fantastic rates, and Mexico steadily grew as a colony of Spain. In contrast, the colonists in North America were concerned with the mere art of survival.

Dr. Strausberg was always fond of saying that while the Pilgrims were starving through their first bitter winter in Plymouth, the Spanish were holding poetry readings in Mexico City. By 1553, Mexico City had established a permanent university and a vast governmental infrastructure. (Crow p. 287) Matched with the material wealth that was flowing out of New Spain, Spanish America seemed to have a bright future.

Two centuries later, the countries had expanded and grown into two vibrant societies with the evolution of distinct cultures. Within fifty years of one another, they would achieve independence from European control. Both broke the bonds that tied them to Europe, and sought to establish a new form of government that they would control. Nevertheless, the way in which both developed was quite different. English North America had undergone a period of benign neglect, so that the colonists learned some self-government. Mexico was still part of the Spanish crown, as was ruled as such.

Even as late as 1846, many in Europe were still putting their faith in the more 'European' Mexico. When the Mexican-American War broke out, American General Winfield Scott sought to carry out a daring overland attack on Mexico City, starting from the port of Vera Cruz.

England's foremost military strategist, the Duke of Wellington, predicted a military disaster for the Americans, stating that "Scott is lost. He cannot capture the city (Mexico City) and he cannot fall back on his base" (Singletary p. 83)

The brilliant capture of Mexico City and the subsequent loss of more than a third of Mexican territory to the United States was forever to change the relationship (and the balance of power) between Mexico and the United States. American, more than ever, started to talk of a Manifest Destiny, stating that all of North America (and for some, the entire Western Hemisphere) was preordained to be ruled by the United States. Some in the United States saw a vast nation that would encompass all the land from Canada in the North to Terra Del Fuego in the South.

Europe, in the guise of the French Emperor Napoleon III, would only dare to meddle in Mexican affairs while Washington was distracted by the Civil War. When the Civil War ended, so did European support for Maximilian's shaky throne. Maximilian would die, bravely, at the hands of the Mexicans he had sought to rule. After 1865, the United States, the new Colossus of the North, eclipsed Mexico. Both had suffered through a brutal and destructive internal struggle, but the United States, specifically the Union states, and the West) underwent a rapid industrialization that would dwarf Mexican efforts.

While United States emerged stronger than ever, Mexico struggled to recover from the revolutions and upheavals it had undergone throughout the 19th Century. Shattered mines and a lack of an established political class would cause Mexico to fall under the control of "strong-men". These were rulers rather than leaders.

This did not mean that Mexico and the Mexicans did not still play important roles in Hemispheric affairs. On the contrary, Mexico had, and still has, a powerful and at times palatable impact on the United States that colors our political debate and effects our relations with our Southern neighbor. It is worth noting that the US diplomatic mission to Mexico, which includes the US Embassy in Mexico City and eight consulates across the rest of Mexico, is the largest diplomatic mission in the world. (Paster p. 61)

Mexico and the United States have a unique social economic and cultural relationship that is unmatched throughout the world. People often speak of the cultural differences between the United States and Canada, but these social variations between the United States and Canada are dwarfed by the differences between Mexico and the United States.

When one goes from Buffalo, New York to Kingston, Ontario for a visit, the differences can be described in subtle shades of gray. While the road signs change and the paper money is a different color; the language and texture of the two countries are still formed from the same bolt of Anglo-Saxon cloth. It is worth noting that Canada is a part of NATO while Mexico is not, and that it fought in World War I and World War II. Mexico too contributed to the Allied war effort in World War II, sending a squadron of bombers to the Pacific to fight in the Philippines. But they did not fight in the scale seen by the Canadians. At Normandy alone, the Canadians suffered thousands of casualties. The cultural links between Canada and the United States have led to economic and diplomatic links that did not develop between the United States and Mexico.

Canada and the United States have a common cultural, religious and political connection to England that is not shared by Mexico. An American or Canadian lawyer can look eastward to London and see clearly the foundations for their law, culture and language. While the laws of Ottawa and Washington evolved into different branches from the laws of London, they can trace their lineage back as to the same source. A Mexican can look east to Madrid, but he also has to look inward to find the remains of Teotihuacan, the seat of Aztec power.

While we may have evolved differently, the United States and Canada share a very common social and ethnic heritage. The line, both physical and cultural, between the United States and Canada is blurred. Most of the radio stations on both sides of the line play the same songs in the same languages. Buffalo, NY and Kingston, ON are not very different cities. However, El Paso, TX and Ciudad Juarez, SO are strikingly different. There is a line; linguistic, religious and cultural, that divides the two more firmly than any cyclone fence could. The United States and Mexico are as different as Japan and Sweden, and yet they share one of the longest boarders in the world.

While so close together, these El Paso and Ciudad Juarez are almost a world apart. Yet their proximity to one another can be seen as the perfect analogy to the relationship between the United States and Mexico. The line that divides the two is the width of a chain- linked fence, or at worst a dirty shallow river, but the social differences form a chasm that will take much effort, from both banks, to bridge.

The destinies of the United States and Mexico are tightly and irrevocably intertwined. Our future can be described as NAFTAesque, as closer integration, fueled by trade, forces us to confront the history between these two nations. In talking of the goals for President Clinton's second term, James Fallows stated that Clinton needed

> [a] dramatic new compact with Mexico. For now the U.S. pretends to control the flow of people, pretends to control the flow of drugs, and pretends that in the long run, the often-unmarked border between these nations will keep them separate.

> Of course, it won't. And a president who wanted to guide the terms on which these societies will inevitably merge could, like Jefferson expanding Westward, say that his country had to plan for peaceful integration with the South. {Fallows)

For the past half-millennium, Mexico and the United States have shared a joined, yet misunderstood history unmatched by any two nations of the world. They are, as see in the title of Alan Riding's work on US-Mexican relations, "Distant Neighbors." The differences between the two, and the scope of their mutual misunderstanding, is great. Writes Riding,

> We share a common border, and common social problems, we are still so far apart, viewing one another with distrust and a long memory. We exist on the same continent, rather than reside as neighbors with one another. At times the tension is palpable. We have tended in recent years to highlight our differences, rather than our similarities. {Riding p. 3)

When there are domestic problems or hard times, both sides are willing to use the other as a symbol of all that is wrong. Cheap Mexican labor is causing unemployment and costing us welfare dollars, claim some in the

United States, while Mexico has never shied away from blaming its economic woes on the United States.

Writes Riding,

> Perhaps nowhere in the world do two countries as different as Mexico and the United States live side by side.... Probably nowhere in the world do two neighbors understand each other so little. More than by levels of development, the two countries are separated by language, religion, race, philosophy and history. The United States is nation barley two hundred years old and it is lunging for the twenty-first century. Mexico is several thousand years old and is still held back by its past. (Riding p. ix)

Americans, (or North Americans, as many in Mexico call us) built a country in a land that was, to the European mind, empty. As far as one could see, there was land, in endless tracts, that took only determination and guns to settle. The land of North America was to prove to some of the most fertile in the world. Indeed the government all but gave away vast tracts of land in the 19th century.

The land belonged to no one (in a European legal sense} so a nation was there for the taking and the making. Mexico is a nation built on the ruins, literally and figuratively, of an ancient empire. In Mexico, there is less good land, and more people are fighting for a small slice on which to live. Any land of value was (and is) available only through the subjugation of others. The size of the Church land holdings plays a role in this area. Frank Tannenbaum wrote of the Church as one of the ten keys to Latin America. The nature of the land (and its ownership) has effected the nature of the people, and how their government has formed. Writes Octivao Paz,

> The history of Mexico is the history of a man seeking his parentage, his origins. He has been influenced at one time or another by

France, Spain, the United States and militant indigenists of his own country, and he crosses history like a jade comet, now and then giving odd flashes of lightning. What is he pursuing in his eccentric course? He wants to go back beyond the catastrophe he suffered. He wants to be the sun again, and to return to the center of that life from which he was separated one day (Paz p. 20)

From this general interest in Mexico, it was simply a matter of choosing a period to study. This period was chosen for three reasons. First, there has not been much research done on this period. People have tended to focus either on the revolution itself, Wilson's adventures in Mexico, or on FDR's Good Neighbor Policy in Latin America. Due the dearth of research on this ten-year period (1917-1927), this represented fertile ground for research. Second, this period is of interest since it represents such as break between the old and the new order. Dwight Morrow represents a sea change in thought and attitude when compared to Henry Lane Wilson. In Mexico itself, Madero and Calles are also of two different epochs. Madero is a product of a 19th century society that would end abruptly in 1914. Calles was a product of that revolution started by Madero. While it may seem unfair to compare the two, it is worth noting that a mere 12 years separates their reigns of power.

The third reason is perhaps the most important. While in the United States we may see this period as only a small part of our global history, it is still a major issue to the Mexican people. Between 1848 and 1916, the United States intervened in Latin America no less than 51 separate times. This tally includes for the Mexican people the loss of 1/3 of her sovereign territory.

It is a memory that reverberates loudly today in Mexico. Everything the United States does to Mexico is viewed through this prism. Until the United States acknowledges the existence of this prism, there will always be problems.

At times the United States has been blind to its own history, and it fails to understand why some people are hostile to what Washington sees as good intentions. The problem is the United States does not have a history in the same sense as China, France or Mexico. China has a history, the United States as a chronicle of current events. When Americans forget their own past, and how others view that past, it runs into problems.

The United States looks at Mexico and at times see poverty and instability. What North Americans do not see is the nation that they invaded 150 years ago and the 30% of sovereign territory they took in conquest. Like a bull lumbering through a china shop, the United States often fails to see the damage that it causes, often unintentionally. What we see as good faith, such as the Monroe Doctrine, is seen as a clear threat by other nations.

In 1981, the Mexican government opened the National Museum of Intervention in Mexico City. While the museum chronicles the action of the French, British and Spanish, it is for the United States that a special place is reserved. The director of the museum, interviewed by the New York Times in 1988, is quoted as saying that "the general tenor of United States foreign policy is interventionist" and that "the theme of intervention continues to be relevant to the present." The museum is designed mainly for Mexican school children, to remind them of their national history. (Rother NYT p. 20) However, history on both sides of the border is affected by this and other perceptions of the history between these two countries. The museum reflects the Mexican perception of the United States. For us to fully understand Mexico, we have to ask ourselves, "why does Mexico feel this way?" and how can we change that perception. That view did not evolve in a vacuum. It is a reflection of our actions.

In his work, Limits to Friendship, Robert Pastor writes that,

Listing to Mexican charges of u.s. 'intervention,' one might conclude that u.s. Marines land in Mexico every third year. In fact, the United States has not intervened militarily in Mexico since its revolution.

Even during this turbulent period from 1910 to 1920, Mexico was hardly an innocent and passive victim of American and European intrigues...Everyone-the Mexican, British and French-tried to use each other for their own purposes. But in the end, the Mexican were more effective in manipulating the foreigners than the other way around. (Pastor Limits to Friendship p. 86)

History has an important place in Mexican life. Americans view history with interest, but much of out effort and energy are spent on looking forward to the future, not backwards to the past. Major events of our history, such as the Mexican-American War, or WWI, are mere sidebars that appeal only to those who study history. For the majority of Americans, Vera Cruz, Okinawa or anyone of a hundred American battlefields is mainly names to be memorized for an exam and then quickly forgotten. North Americans constantly talk about the future, while Mexicans are always referring back to the past.

The general public in this nation would be hard pressed to give a coherent discussion of the Spanish American War, or even when it occurred. The Mexican-American War, which in its time generated as much protest as the Vietnam war a century later, is treated as one of those "19th century" wars, like the Franco-Prussian War or the Boer War. Only slightly better than the dustbin of history, home of rejected ideas, is the file cabinet of history, home of forgotten wars and dead white males. Writes Abraham Lowenthal,

North Americans generally favor closer relations with Mexico; they typically assume that the interests of Mexico and the United States are easily compatible. Many Mexicans, however, think the relationship is inevitably exploitative. The perspectives Mexicans and North Americans bring to bear on specific issues often differ fundamentally. Insensitivity from the North and hypersensitivity from the South frequently convert simple differences into great difficulties. (Lowenthal P. 79)

In Mexico however, the past is always made part of the present. Actions taken today are viewed, and distorted, the kaleidoscope of yesterday's experiences. In the United States, commentators on the Gulf War in 1991 could not talk of the impending battle without drawing parallels with Vietnam. We saw actions today though the history of the past. But in some way we keep the two separate, while in Mexican perceptions of history, the two are irrevocably intertwined.

In a similar way, Mexicans cannot talk about trade with North American without also talking about Vera Cruz or the exploitative policies of North American oil companies. The difference is that the Mexicans have a lot more history to talk about behind them, and the centuries run together, giving a Mexican perspective. Writes Riding,

> The past remains alive in the Mexican soul. History, revised and adjusted to suit contemporary needs, is therefore mobilized to maintain the cohesion of modern society. When ancient and modern clash, emotions invariably favor the past. In late 1983, the mayor of Mexico City was forced to cancel plans to build a subway line under the capital's main plaza after angry protests..... that construction would destroy hidden remains of the Aztec Empire: the only surprise was that the mayor had lacked the sensitivity to avoid the controversy. Compared to the past, urban planning in unimportant. One explanation for this constant reliving of the past is that honor and glory must somehow be extracted from dizzying array of defeats and humiliations suffered by Mexicans since the Conquest. (Riding p.21-22)

Perhaps the complex, and at time contradictory feelings of Mexicans can best be summed up by one of its greatest authors. Writes Octivao Paz,

For more than a century, that country has appeared to our eyes as a gigantic but scarcely human reality. Smiling or angry, its hand clenched or open, the United States neither sees nor hears us, but keeps striding on, and as it does, enters our land and crushes us. It is impossible to hold back a giant. It is possible, though far from easy, to make him listen to others. If he listens, this opens the possibility of co-existence. (p. 95 Faster Limits to Friendship)

One only has to look to the steep and rugged mountains of the Mexican State of Chiapas to see that the history of Mexico lives in the present day. Under the banner of Emilano Zapata, the Zapatistas, led by sub-commandate Marcos, are continuing the struggle for peasant land rights started by Zapata eight decades earlier. The way to the future in Mexico is under the banner of the past. That a communal model of land ownership has been seen as failure in capitalist systems of the West is entirely irrelevant.

The idea of communal lands for peasants espoused by Zapata still holds great appeal for the indigenous people of Southeastern Mexico. It was the rally cry in 1911, and will be the rally cry in 1998. Time is less important than the perception.

By looking to the past, Mexicans seek to find a path to the future. To understand Mexico, one needs to look at her history and to try and understand it from the Mexican perspective. One can not just read the dry facts of Mexican history; one has to learn how Mexicans interpret that history. The people of the United States are not a history minded people; we have not been around long enough to be so. We have always looked for what is new, and to see how we can expand, ever westward.

We look to Asia for our trade, we look to the west for expansion from 1789 on, and we look forward to the future, not back to the past. Mexicans seek to gain understanding from the past, to somehow achieve some understanding of who they are. Americans seek, in large part, only inspiration. People do not want to discuss the fine points of what caused World War II. What is important in the United States is simply that we won, and that our cause was just. This is not say that this viewpoint is right or wrong; only that this is the way things exist.

To understand, in part, the key players in this drama, one has to understand the way in which they view history. In the simplest terms, Mexicans look to the past while the United States looks to the future. One only has to listen to the theme of President Clinton, as he seeks to build a "Bridge to the 21st Century." One of the joys of American political speech is that "themes" do not have to have a very deep meaning. Many would be hard pressed to define what a bridge to the 21st century exactly means. For the concerns of this paper, it simply serves to illustrate the forward thinking nature of Americans.

Editorial Method

▼

This book was first written on a Pentium 100 computer using WordPerfect 7.0. It was revised an updated on an AMD K6-III 350 using Appleworks 5.0, and then exported out to a Microsoft Word 97 format for publication. The paper was written using Times New Roman set to a font size of 10, with full justification.

CHRONOLOGY

---▼---

This work was started in the fall of 1996, with the majority of the research being done between December of 1996 and December of 1997. It was put aside, untouched from 1997 until the fall of 2000, when it was taken in had for revision and formatting for publication. It is in many ways an unfinished work. Time prevents me from doing a full revision of the book, but this work serves as a foundation for the work I wanted to write.

INTRODUCTION

---▼---

The period of relations from 1910-1917 between Mexico and the United States can be divided into two distinct phases. The first spans from 1910-1917, when the United States was most concerned with physical security along the border. It was in this period that most of the fighting took place in the North of Mexico.

It was at this time that Americans, both in Mexico and along the border, feared for their safety. A number of clashes between rival Mexican forces in towns bordering the US led to accidental shootings of Americans on the US side. It was also in this period that Pancho Villa carried out his raid into Columbus, New Mexico, which brought about the Pershing expedition.

The second period of diplomatic relations (and the focus of this paper) spans from 1917-1923, when the physical threat to the welfare of Americans had been greatly diminished. Rather, the threat to the United States was perceived in economic terms, as American financial interests, especially oil companies faced the threat of confiscatory taxes or direct expropriation of their property by the post-revolutionary Mexican government. This threat of economic ruin stemmed directly from the promulgation in 1917 of a new, and for its time radical, Mexican Constitution.

This new constitution radically changed the manner and scale in which foreign companies were allowed to operate in Mexico, as subsoil rights and labor relations were codified into Mexican national law, giving Mexicans a new view of themselves and their economic power.

It was to be Article 27, more than any other, that was to color relations between Mexico and the United States in this period. The constitution of 1917 writes Parkes, meant, "the ideals of the Revolution had been written into the fundamental laws of the country" (Parkes p. 362) The means in which Mexico sought to enact these laws has affected relations to this very day. Article 27, and how the Mexican government sought to enforce it, is in large part a focus of this paper. Due to the nature of Mexican law, the Article itself was not enough to take over foreign owned wells. Under Mexican law, each amendment required enabling legislation to bring it into force.

This struggle to enforce Article 27 will form in large part the framework of the differences between the United States and Mexico in this period. How Mexico would control its destiny, and what, if anything, the United States would to change that destiny, is the question this work seeks to answer.

CHAPTER ONE

1917

1917 was to prove to be an important year in the formation of American foreign policy. The Villa Expedition of 1916, under General Pershing, was withdrawn unilaterally by Woodrow Wilson, as the threat of war with Imperial Germany loomed large on the horizon. The threat from Mexican instability was seen to wane in light of the greater threat of Prussian militarism. A fight for the future of Europe overshadowed the troubles on the Southern border. Many of the concerns of Wilson and others in Washington about Mexico were put aside as the Allied powers faced the threat of a resurgent Imperial Germany, which sought to force the issue by resuming unrestricted submarine warfare. Given the collapse of the forces of the Tsar on the eastern front, Germany was now in a race to get troops to the western front before the United States got into the war.

This was a gamble on the part of Germany; her hope was that she could deny the Allies of enough supplies before the United States could become fully involved in the war effort. While the United States withdrew from

Mexico, this did not end the threat of conflict. It is just that the threat from Mexico paled when compared to the threat of Prussian militarism.

Indeed, there would be times over the ten years that followed that the threat of intervention was to be raised by some in the United States, but never carried through. This work will seek to examine these threats, and why, ultimately, they were never carried out.

While this work will examine the actions of both the United States and Mexico, the emphasis will be on the actions of the United States leadership in its dealings with the various governments of Mexico from 1917-1927. Ultimately, the United States chose diplomacy over force. The question we seek to answer is why.

Although there were many major political issues between the United States and Mexico in this period, one of the driving factors between the two nations was economic. The United States had invested millions in the development of Mexican resources between 1890-1910, and had substantial holdings to protect. Brutal warfare between Mexican factions threatened the physical security of these holdings, as battles raged back and forth across Mexico. In addition to the threats of combat, there was also the specter of political actions, mainly in the form of direct expropriation of foreign holdings. Much had been spent in developing Mexico, and few were willing to give it up without a fight.

American Capital investments in mines, railroads and telegraphs all faced destruction by combat by rival Mexican factions. American firms had spent time and capital to develop the infrastructure necessary to develop (or exploit, depending on your vantage point) the natural resources of Mexico. Throughout this period, American companies would go to pains to point out that it was they, and not the Mexicans, who developed the oil fields and transportation infrastructure of Mexico.

The American companies would also spend great effort in pointing out that all of their economic development was carried out under the auspices of the Mexican laws then in force at the time of development. Americans would take a procedural, legal approach that their rights in Mexico were being violated, and they would turn to Mexican courts to try to achieve redress for their grievances, and try to protect their interests as best they could under the Mexican system.

But the legalistic outcome of the Mexican Revolution, the Mexican Constitution of 1917, threatened the de jure security of these holdings. The relations between Mexico and the United States were to be shadowed by the threat of Mexican jurisprudence, not Mexican arms. Control of, and access to, Mexican natural resources would be at the center of this conflict.

A secondary topic of concern throughout this period was to be physical security of the borders. Throughout this period, the United States was express concern of the security of the border areas. It was not so much a fear of war with Mexico, than with Mexican irregulars letting the battle splash over onto American territory. While Villa's 1916 raid on Columbus, NM was the most spectacular; there were numerous incidents of fighting between Mexican factions that inadvertently involved the United States.

All of these issues combined to make relations between the two countries difficult at best. Neither side made a strong attempt to try to understand the position (or concerns) of the other. Suspicion, rather than confidence building (to use the modern term) was to be a major theme on both sides of the Rio Grande. It would not be until the 1930's that the relationship would improve to the level seen before 1910.

It would be World War II that was to bring the United States closer to Mexico, and would ironically lay the foundations for some of the problems in the post-war period. In World War II, Mexican aviators fought alongside the United States, fighting the Japanese in the Philippines.

Mexican U.S. Relations -1910-1917

It is somewhat ironic that in 1910, US-Mexican relations were quite cordial. Provide Diaz, the ruler of Mexico, had established under his rule a stable Mexico with a business environment that fostered foreign investment. The United States had become a major investor in Mexican industry, and relations between the two nations were the best they had been in more than fifty years. The bitterness felt by the Mexicans in the wake of the Mexican-American War of 1848 had faded in the intervening fifty years. American foreign policy actions in the Western Hemisphere did not endear Washington to most Latin Americans, but relations were civil. Writes Karl Schmitt,

> During the 30-year period from 1880-1910, Mexican United States relations revolved not around political disputes or military threats as in previous decades, but around economic issues.... During these years both countries concentrated their energies on reconstruction following destructive internal strife. (Schmitt p.97)

It was not the desire for more land by the Americans, but rather the control of key sectors of the economy in Mexico, where they could control both production and price. Writes Schmitt, "US ambitions towards Mexico changed from territorial expansion to economic penetration" (Schmitt p. 110)

In 1897, American investment in Mexico totaled $ 200 million dollars. In only five years, this investment had risen to $ 500 million, spread across 1,117 companies and individuals. (Callahan p. 510) By 1912, American investment had risen to $ 1,500 million dollars. (Meyer p. 10) In the fields where Americans had invested, they tended to dominate these sectors of the economy. Americans controlled 78% of the mines, 72% of the smelters, 58% of oil production and 68% of the rubber business. (Callahan p. 519)

Most of this investment occurred after 1877, with more than half of this investment coming after 1896. When Diaz was able to consolidate his base of power in Mexico, he made the business climate favorable to foreign investment. Modifications to Mexican mineral laws fostered a legal environment where American companies were willing to invest in the infrastructure necessary to develop drilling and mining in Mexico.

As a sign of the improved relations between Mexico and the United States, President Taft initiated a meeting in 1909. Taft met Diaz on October 16, 1909 at the international boundary near El Paso. Taft proposed the meeting as a means of informally celebrating the increasingly cordial relations between the two countries. It also served to signal that Mexico and the United States could co-exist with one another.

The meeting was noteworthy since it was the fist time that a sitting President was to leave the United States during his term of office. For Diaz, it was a great political success, as he saw it as an affirmation of his position as leader of Mexico by the great Colossus of the North. Diaz appeared in all his regal and imperial splendor, while Taft appeared plain in a business suit when standing next to the be-medalled general.

Much of the new investment was in the infant Mexican oil industry that was developing at the turn of the century. Railroads still dominated American investment, but after the turn of the century, new investments were increasingly channeled into the emerging petroleum industry in Mexico. Oil was also different from railroads and telegraphs, as both the product and the money flowed out of the country. Oil was also seen as the one commodity other than gold and silver that could make Mexico wealthy once again, and give it some control over its future. The value of these Mexican oil fields greatly increased after 1914, as the war in Europe spurred a great demand for oil and gasoline. The rising value of Mexican oil exports gave Americans a greater influence in Mexico, as the majority of the oil fields were run or financed by the United States. It was not the direct control of resource, but control of their exploitation that mattered.

Oil is important, since it formed both the political and social foundation for much of the diplomatic conflict between Mexico and the United States during this period. It is not the only monetary issue of the oil itself, but also for what oil represented to both the Mexican nation and to American industrialists. How Americans and Mexicans view oil is indicative of how each side viewed natural resources and their exploitation.

To the United States, oil was a commodity, like any other, that was to be developed and exploited. The growth of American industry demanded ever high levels of oil to fuel its expansion and Americans soon looked Southward for new sources of oil. With the start of World War One, oil was to become a strategic resource that would have to be protected, at all costs, in order to fuel the Allied war effort in Europe and on the Atlantic. To the Mexicans, oil was a natural treasure being extracted by the United States, with the profits from that extraction also going to the United States. For the Mexicans, this was an issue of national honor, as others were controlling the path of Mexico's development, and getting rich along the way. This was simply one more example of how wealth was leaving Mexico to enrich another country, another example of Mexico's exploitation.

In the 16th century, it was silver and gold flowing to Madrid; in the 20th century, it was oil flowing to American industry. Both represented the exploitation of Mexico by a foreign power, to which Mexico had little recourse. American petroleum development in Mexico brought about a reaction from Mexicans that was not seen with the development of the railroads. Part of this stems from the perception of oil as a resource that was physically and allegorically leaving the country, along with all the profits.

Between 1901-1911, oil production in Mexico leapt from a mere 10,345 barrels of oil to 12,552,798 barrels of oil. Between 1911-1918, oil production would jump even higher, as shown in below (Meyer p. 8).

But the American presence was not completely one- sided as exploiters of resources. American investment provided jobs in Mexico, and also allowed for the development of capital infrastructures, such as railroads and port facilities. Under the stability of the Diaz regime, Mexico experienced a great period of modernization and expansion of its industry and infrastructure. With the achievement of political and economic stability, railroads and telegraph lines quickly radiated across Mexico, fueled by American capital. By 1915, American investment was increasingly being concentrated in the oil industry, as domestic use and European war demands for fuel and lubricants necessitated the search for new (and controllable) sources of oil. While neutral, the United States provided much of the oil was used to fuel the Allied war machine.

The Creelman Interview

In February of 1908, Diaz granted an interview to the American journalist James Creelman of Pearson's Magazine. In this interview, Diaz stated that he was not going to seek another term as the President of Mexico, and that he would welcome and support the formation of active political parties in Mexico. For a man who had ruled for a good part of the 19th century, this was news to many, especially those in Mexico.

This interview would not be seen in Mexico for a month, when it appeared as a translation in a Mexico City newspaper. It is only then that most Mexicans saw the potential that this announcement had for the future of Mexico. This article created a stir among those who felt they could lay claims to the keys of the empire.

By the time article appeared in translation, Diaz started to withdraw from this position. While Diaz did not openly repudiate what he said in the interview, he did try to downplay the importance of the interview, insofar as it related to Mexican politics and the future of Mexico. He tried to pass it off, unsuccessfully, as a passing idea of little importance (or relevance) to Mexico or the Mexican political system.

Diaz had hoped that Mexican publican opinion, such that existed, would rise up as a single voice to protest the proposed retirement of Diaz. When Mexicans expressed no desire for Diaz to run again, and actively welcomed the idea of change, he was left in a somewhat awkward position. It was finally resolved, at least for Diaz, when he stated that he had been "convinced" that he needed to run again for President. There have been a variety of explanations put forth for the Creelman interview, but the most logical seems to be that Diaz meant the article only for American consumption. By March of 1908 however, it was clear that he had committed a major political mistake. There was little protest over Diaz's reversal of his position, but his announcement did unleash a great deal of private political activity in Mexico. At the age of 78, no one expected that Diaz would live to see the end of an eighth six-year term of office in 1916. The political struggle therefore centered on who would become the vice- presidential candidate. This issue of age is important, as it defines, for some, the real root causes of the Mexican Revolution. Diaz and the state governors under his control were all in their seventies or older, and had held a grip on the reigns of Mexican politics since the 1870s. This is significant for a country where the life expectancy for a male was but 27 years. (Atkins p. 42)

While the official PRI party line is that the Mexican Revolution was an agrarian revolution, it has been suggested by many that the immediate cause was a struggle within the power elite between older, entrenched politicos and young, ambitious men who tired of waiting and wanted their shot at power before they became too old. As Dr. Strausberg was fond of stating, "the train was full."

CHAPTER TWO

▼

THE MEXICAN REVOLUTION

Diaz, once he announced his intention to run again, found no shortage of ambitious men who had a thirst for power. There slowly evolved a loosely aligned opposition movement to Diaz, led in large part by Francisco Indalecio Madero, a wealthy land owner from the North of Mexico. Madero's popularity rose directly from a book he wrote in 1908, called The Presidential Succession of 1910. From an editorial standpoint, the book was a dry tome, which plowed through a political discourse on Mexican history.

The book was to a have a great impact however, as Madero attacked the Diaz system without attacking Diaz himself. Madero made it quite clear in the work that he was advocating a peaceful succession of Presidential power as delineated in the existing but widely ignored Constitution of 1857. Madero's rallying cry was to be "effective suffrage, no reelection.

It is one of the great ironies of Mexican history that Madero, a man who denounced revolution as the solution to Mexico's problems, would be the catalyst for a series intermittent revolutions that sweep Mexico from

1910- 1917. This Revolutionary period, called a "fiesta with bullets" would cost Mexico more than 2% of her population, and would forever alter the face of Mexican politics.

This Revolution, although less well known than the Bolshevik Revolution of 1917, was to have a lasting impact on Mexican society that is still felt today. One could also argue that the Mexican revolution became, regardless of its origin, a true peasant struggle for power against the ruling oligarchy of state, aristocrat and Church. More than the Russian, Chinese or Cuban revolutions, the Mexican revolution, regard- less of its origin, brought change from the bottom. All the other quickly established a ruling elite, mainly in the form of Politburos, which con- trolled the reigns of power.

Writes Selman Rodman,

> [I]n terms of our century, the Mexican revolution of 1910-1924 enjoys a special primacy. It was the first successful peasant uprising against a landed oligarchy. It was the first nationwide proletarian revolt against industrial capitalism, and it was the first revolt against Big power imperialism on the part of an underdeveloped country. As such, it influenced the later Russian Revolution to a considerable extent. And its "positive" consequences-social secu- rity, joint capital- labor management, agriculture under partial control of the farm-producers' cooperative, and in embryo all the features of the welfare state- have been a generic part of the evolu- tion of most Western societies ever since. (Rodman p. 96)

Madero was to be the catalyst for the Mexican Revolution, but was opposed to violent revolution. Indeed, Madero's call to arms, known as The Plan of San Luis Potosi, was more parliamentary than revolutionary. Madero called for reestablishment of the Mexican Constitution of 1857. He had himself named provisional president, and planned for a presiden- tial election after Diaz's overthrow had been achieved. It was Madero's goal to simply remove Diaz from power, not to start a revolution in Mexico. Indeed, everything Madero said pointed to a desire to work within the system, not to overthrow it. Madero wrote {and issued) the Plan of San Luis Potosi from Texas and called for the revolt to start on November 20, 1910. The plans fell into the hands of Mexican Federal troops and the Revolution got off to a shaky start. At first it looked as though the revolt was going to fail under Madero, but momentum grew when Villa, fighting in the North, started to capture towns from Federal forces.

At the same time, Emilano Zapata brought the revolt forward in the southern state of Morelos, uniting the peasants in demands for land redistribution. With his early success, he pushed uncomfortably close the Mexico City, threatening the stability of Diaz's regime. This was to be the foundation of a major problem that was to plague the entire revolutionary period. It had produced many leaders of prominence, but they had widely divergent, and at times conflicting, goals for the Mexican Revolution. With no one leader to unite the people, the various factions wasted their effort and treasure fighting each other instead of rebuilding Mexico. The Mexican Revolution never produced a Lenin, Mao or Castro, and was to suffer from the lack of charismatic, central leader.

There was Madero, the moderate who wished to change the leadership of Mexico, rather than the underlying political system. Fighting in the North of Mexico was Villa, with a reputation for bravery and brutality, speaking for the poor through the barrel of gun who wished to rise against their oppressive landlords. In the South, there was Zapata, another warrior for the landless, disenfranchised, peasants who had the polish that Villa lacked.

In the words of Ronald Atkins, Zapata was

"[A] Communist who had never heard of Communism, he fought relentlessly and mercilessly for the rights of the poor. Peasants by the thousands rallied to his stirring cry, 'Men of the South, it is better to die on your feet than live on your knees'" (Atkins 54-55)

These three main leaders, with highly incompatible goals, and the means for achieving them, soon came to crossed swords. Diaz was forced from power in the May of 1911, and Madero was to stumble along, with a tenuous grip, as president until 1913. Madero failed, in large part, because the desires of the people, which found a voice under Zapata and villa, far exceeded the reforms that Madero had proposed in The Plan of San Luis Potosi. The times had simply passed Madero to move onto the 20th century, as he was unwilling to fully embrace the changes demanded by the forces of the Revolution that he had unleashed.

Madero soon lost favor with other elements of the Mexican Revolution. Madero was unwilling (or unable) to radicalize the Mexican revolution, which he saw as finished with the departure of Diaz. Villa and Zapata both felt that Madero had failed to implement the full potential of the Mexican Revolution. Madero, by trying to maintain a middle of the road approach, had succeeded only in getting run over by men who were willing to use force and terror to achieve their goals.

CHAPTER THREE

▼

THE OVERTHROW OF MADERO

In November of 1911, no sooner had Madero taken office than Zapata issued the Plan of Ayala, which called for the restoration of Indian lands taken from them by the large haciendas. In the word of John Womack, the plan of Ayala stemmed from the Morelos peasant chiefs being "disgusted with the government's academic attitude towards "the agrarian question…[they] formally denounced Madero" (Bethell Mexico since Independence p. 136).

The Plan of Ayala endorsed the basic framework of Madero's Plan of San Luis Potosi, and then made a major amendment that was to change the course and direction of the Mexican Revolution. In part, the Plan of Ayala stated that,

> We proclaim, be it known: that lands, woods and waters usurped by the hacendados, cientificos or caciques though tyranny and venal justice henceforth belong to the towns or citizens who have corresponding titles to these properties, of which they were despoiled by

the bad faith of our oppressors. They shall retain possession of the said properties at all costs, arms in hand. (Keen p. 323)

Madero now faced not only political revolution, which could be stanched with reforms, but a threat of social revolution, which sought to tear at the already fragile fabric of Mexico. Madero simply did not have the ability or the force of will to lead through the great upheavals of the Mexican Revolution.

Madero was able to weather four rebellions in his short time in office. These rebellions were led by Bernardo Reyes, Pazcual Orzco and Felix Diaz. Madero was finally he was done in by a joint rebellion of Reyes and Diaz. The final defeat of Madero however, would not come from rebels on the outside of his government, but from forces within, as Madero turned to one of his generals to fend off the assault of Diaz and Reyes, and he would be betrayed. Writes Lesley Byrd Simpson, the greatest mistake made by Madero was that "he did not shoot his prisoners" (Many Mexico's p. 299). Misplaced trusts, combined with an inability to act forcefully, were to undo Madero's very short reign of power. But this not to deny Madero's role in starting the Mexican Revolution.

Whatever his failings as the leader of an increasingly radical rebellion, Madero planted the seeds for social and political change in Mexico. He had awoken a sleeping populace, and they were now hungry for change. Writes Rodman,

It is still not recognized, and perhaps least of all in Mexico itself, that Francisco I. Madero was the real hero of the Mexican Revolution. The other leaders in the great drama, with their sanctioning of various forms of social extermination, did the obvious in terms of self- interest. Madero alone acted against his personal and class interest, believing in the rights of all men, and in principle. (Rodman P. 97)

Madero's betrayal from within came at the hands of General Victoriano Huerta, who had put down Orozco's rebellion. After crushing Orozco, he had been dismissed by Madero over concerns of questionable accounting in his command. Madero had little choice however, when faced with the Reyes-Diaz rebellion, and he turned to Huerta to crush the rebellion.

Reyes was killed in the first day of fighting, giving Madero a sense that he had weathered another rebellious storm. But the battle between the two sides flared up when the rebels discovered that the centrally located Citadel, which served as an armory for Mexico City, was lightly defended. It was quickly seized, giving new life to the rebellion. The ensuing combat between the two sides centered on downtown Mexico City, where Diaz had his forces were in the Citadel, and the forces of Huerta were in the National Palace, less than a mile away.

What was to follow was to be known as the Ten Terrible Days (February 8-18, 1913), as both sides shelled each other, ineffectually killing few troops on the other side, but hundreds of civilians who lived in the 3/4 of a mile between the two targets. The citizens of Mexico City, for the first time, saw the battle that accompanied the Mexican Revolution.

Prior to this, combat had been limited to the countryside, and had not touched most urban Mexicans directly. The people of Mexico City now saw the battle and carnage that had ravished the Mexican countryside since 1910. The capital now became the central battleground for the latest phase of the Mexican Revolution. It was here that the revolution entered its most brutal stage, and would effect how the United States was to view Mexico for the next decade. The killing only ended with the intervention of Henry Lane Wilson, Taft's ambassador to Mexico. Ambassador Wilson worked out an agreement known as the Pact of the Citadel, which was to place Huerta in charge of Mexico. Huerta received American support since he was seen by Ambassador Wilson as able to restore order to Mexico. Ambassador Wilson extracted a pledge from Huerta, stating that Madero and his family would be allowed to leave the country to go into exile, as Diaz had in 1911. The promise from Huerta lasted all of three days, as Madero and his Vice-President were killed "while trying to escape." It became clear that while Huerta would work for American interests, he was not going to keep his enemies around if he had any say in the matter. It would seem, at the time, a good idea to eliminate one's opposition. Keeping Madero alive could give Huerta little benefit, and could only cause problems for him later on.

While the killing of one's political enemies and rivals has a long history in Mexico, the death of Madero was to have long ranging implications for Mexico and the United States. It was to serve as the touchstone for all that was to follow. Writes Rodman,

> [t]he aimless confrontation could have had comic-opera aspects but for two factors. The nobility of the President's character, his bravery, and his naiveté, were now transparent. The infamy of the American ambassador, who was now working night and day to trap for him the drunken Huerta in a spider's web of false claims and hypocritical appeals, was not revealed until later. What Henry Lane Wilson managed to bring about in those ten days of intrigue was far more reprehensible than what the American armies had done to Mexico in 1847, where the struggle for power had been quite open and Mexico's leaders had been corrupt and treacherous. (Rodman p. 107)

Had Huerta allowed Madero to simply go into exile, chances are quite good he would have remained in power will little difficulty or interference from the United States. He would have simply been another Latin American strongman for the United States to take into account and reach some sort of accord. While many talk of his inability to govern Mexico, he was in reality a savvy leader with a keen political sense. His only mistake and the one that would cost him power, was having Madero and his brother killed, and doing it without any attempt at being subtle.

Madero was facing challenges from many sections of the country, and Huerta was simply the one who acted first. In their work entitled *Victoriano Huerta a reappraisal*, William Sherman and Richard Greenleaf write that,

> Venustiano Carranza, who later overthrew the Huerta regime, probably had been on the point of rising against Madero. In addition, it has been seen that the Madero administration faced revolts by Reyes, Orozco, and Felix Diaz, besides the continued ravaging carried on by Zapata and number of less prominent revolutionaries.
> (Sherman and Greenleaf P. 73)

Madero was, at best, a mediocre and naive political leader. He had neither the will nor the force of personality to lead Revolutionary Mexico. He was not beloved by his followers, like Villa and Zapata were, nor was he feared as Diaz had been. Madero was from the middle of the road, and he lacked the means to enforce his will and his position upon Mexico. He sought only to effect a transition in government, but in the process opened a Pandora's box. All the aspirations of Mexico, urban and rural, peasant and intellectual sprang forth after years of being subsumed to the will of Diaz. Madero was not equal to the task, but he deserves recognition for trying to better the system. His biggest failing seems to be his naiveté. Writes Skidmore,

> Madero was hardly a true revolutionary. He was a would- be parliamentarian who thought Diaz's abdication would open the way to true democracy. Madero belonged in England or Scandinavia, not Mexico. He flinched at the thought-suggested to him by less squeamish rebels-that he should strike at his opposition, before they struck at him. (Skidmore p. 230)

While he was not beloved by his people, he was neither hated. His death allowed a populace who was at best lukewarm to him in life to lionize him and turned him into a martyr. In death, the prophet Madero became the loss of all Mexico could have become, of her most promising, and democratic, future. Madero's legacy is that he risked his privileged status to try to right what he saw as wrongs in the Mexican system. What he may have lacked in the ability to rule was more than made up in the risk he took to try and say his country. More than the other revolutionary leaders, Madero went against the interest of his class in an attempt to build a better Mexico for all Mexicans. Huerta made the one error (albeit major) mistake of having Madero killed, and underestimating the response of the world to his actions. In addition to poor judgment in killing Madero, Huerta suffered from poor timing. Within days of taking power, Huerta's actions were to be called to task by the more orderly (and for him ominous} transfer of power north of the Rio Grande. The political changing of the guard in the colossus of the North was to have a severe impact on the future of Mexico and Huerta.

CHAPTER FOUR

WOODROW WILSON AND THE MEXICAN PROBLEM

The inauguration of Woodrow Wilson was to bring about a marked change in how the United States was to conduct its foreign affairs. Wilson, with a strong missionary streak, was appalled by Huerta's actions and he was firm in his conviction that such a usurpation of power would not be rewarded with American recognition. Huerta, who had cut a deal with Taft's ambassador Wilson, was perplexed by the American actions. Woodrow Wilson brought a strong evangelical streak to the White House, and he saw the death of Madero as a subversion of the "democratic" process in Mexico. Wilson was going to impart proper democratic ideals of the Mexicans, whether they wanted them or not. Wilson stated that he "would teach the Latin American republics to elect good men."

With little regard for the nature of Mexican society (or the Mexicans themselves) and no small measure of American arrogance, Wilson sought to impose "the correct solution" on Mexico from the outside as though he were dealing with surely school boys. This idea that democracy could be transplanted like a sapling was naive, and was to make Mexico a quagmire that drained Wilson's efforts over the next eight years. Wilson never comes close to his goals for Mexico.

This was a new approach in American foreign policy. Taft had no real qualms about Huerta, but considered withholding recognition until the Mexicans were willing to negotiate over existing boundaries disputes between the two countries. Taft saw withholding recognition as a negotiating lever, rather than an opportunity to impose some moral dictate on Mexico. Writes P. Edward Haley,

> Taft's policy possessed the well-defined objectives and rather strict limits on the use of force peculiar to his understanding of the national interest and could have dictated that most far-reaching military involvement in Mexico, a contiguous country where American investments were large. In the case of Mexico, the restraints on Taft's actions arose from the calm and patient manner in which he implemented his principles rather than from the principles themselves. The advantage of Taft's response to revolution, like the approach to foreign relations from which it proceeded, was that it forbade involvement or at least military involvement in countries whose welfare does not affect America's economic and security interests, strictly defined. (Haley p. 261)

Wilson, on the other hand, took a very different approach, and one that was to bring him nothing but grief in his many dealing with Mexico. The Mexican policy of the Wilson administration was designed to be proactive, and correct what it perceived as a moral wrong. Given the naive, textbook foundations of its political assumptions, it was doomed to failure. Wilson could no more impose a representative democracy on Mexico than England could impose a functioning parliamentary system on Czarist Russia.

The policy sought to impose Wilson's political beliefs on a system where it simply would not work. With little regard for the history of Mexico, Wilson sought to impose an American democracy on a nation with no experience in representative government.

Wilson made the same mistake that was to be made in 1919 at the Paris Peace Conference. Just as you could not impose a democratic system on Weimar Germany, you could not just make Mexico a democracy just because it seemed like a good idea. It could take generations for democracy to take root, and all the good intentions can not move it along any faster. Writes Samuel Bemis,

> Woodrow Wilson's Mexican policy, based on his principle of not recognizing a usurper's overthrow of constitutional government, can hardly be called an unqualified success. He intervened diplomatically to save the Mexican people from a new dictator. This novel action, the product of idealism and inexperience, involved him against his will in limited military interventions, and it very nearly brought the United States into an unnecessary war at an extraordinarily critical moment of its history. He open full wide the sluiceway of a revolution that distressed and ravaged the people beyond measure. P. 189

Wilson, in an attempt to impose "proper" government on Mexico, served only to enflame the chaos that had until that point been subsiding in Mexico. Bemis' criticism of Wilson's policy is shared by others. The problem was that it is difficult to convert theory into practice under the best conditions, and Mexico did not led itself to such applications of theory. Writes Robert Quirk,

> The Latin Americans-and particularly the Mexicans-would be led by the nose into Zion, a Wilsonian political paradise bounded on one side by the ideals of the eighteenth century

philosophers, and on the other side by stern Calvinist piety. If Wilson's Mexican policy was a failure, which by all accounts it was, it was precisely because he never lost his magisterial air in dealing with those he considered his inferiors (Quirk p. 2)

Wilson's failure to create an effective policy for dealing with the Mexicans stems in large part from his inability to understand them. Wilson, rightfully distrustful of Ambassador Henry Lane Wilson, sought to place his own "special emissaries" in Mexico.

These two emissaries, William Bayard Hale and George Lind, were to advise Wilson on how to deal with Mexico, and come up with viable solutions. A situation that would require many experts was given to men who's only qualification was tell Wilson what he wanted to hear.

Neither had an understanding of Mexico or of it's political system, and they served only to give Wilson confusing and inaccurate information on the situation in Mexico. These emissaries had little contact with the Mexican government, and used the American community in Mexico as a source for almost all of their information. They served Wilson poorly, and exacerbated an already difficult situation. Writes Barbara Tuchman of Hale,

> His qualification for the mission consisted in knowing nothing whatever about Mexico but a good deal about Wilson. A quick glance around was all he needed to report back what he knew Wilson wanted to hear: that Huerta was indeed the archfiend, that his regime could not last (Tuchman p. 42)

Wilson's other choice. John Lind faired little better. Seeking to find what Wilson wanted to hear, rather than seeking the truth, were to color the actions of Lind and Hale in Mexico. In the process, they did a great disservice to both countries, and set the cause of peace back many years in the process. Writes Simpson of Lind,

The envoy, John Lind, was a well-meaning but heavy- handed man, with no Spanish, and contemptuous and arrogant besides. Lind infuriated Huerta and the Mexican Foreign Minister, the able Federico de Gamboa, by repeating Wilson's threat to withhold recognition unless Huerta should step down and call a general election, in which Huerta should not be a candidate. (Simpson p. 302- 303)

In addition to their heavy handedness, the actions of Lind and Hale in Mexico may have been counterproductive. The nature of Mexican elections is such that reality and perception are often quite different. Martin Needler, in his work, Latin American Politics in Perspective, states that the manner in which a elections occur in the United States and how they occur elsewhere can be quite different. Writes Needler,

By one means or another, imposicion, the imposition on the voters of an "official" candidate, regardless of their preferences, is a general practice. In the entire history of several of the republics no Presidential candidate sponsored by the incumbent administration has ever been defeated in a popular election. This has been on occasion been because he was in reality the popular choice, of course. Because of the prevalence of imposicion, it is not enough to assume that a President who traces his title to a popular election is a legitimate democrat, whereas one who came to power through a revolt is a dictatorial usurper. The popular election in question mat have been thoroughly rigged, whereas the revolt may have been a genuine expression of the popular will, forced to take the path of revolt because it had been frustrated by the corruption of the electoral process. Woodrow Wilson's policies frequently came to grief because of his failure to understand this point. (Needler p. 144)

At first, Huerta was able to retain power by working with British oil interests, who were in fierce competition with American oil concerns for the petroleum deposits being developed. Huerta may have been vilified by some in the American press, be he was not without those who supported his efforts.

Huerta had come into power with the collusion of Ambassador Wilson, and he had support from within the Mexican Army. In addition, Huerta had the support of those who wanted to undo the social changes made since 1910. Huerta was, in the strictest sense of the word, a counter revolutionary. He was going to restore order in Mexico, which meant a return to business as usual. Writes George Creel,

> Huerta was by no means friendless. In his corruption and brutality, the forces of privilege saw rare opportunity for the restoration of a regime as profitable as that of Diaz, and all the resources of power and wealth, both in and outside Mexico, were put behind the usurper. Ambassador Wilson, as his part, set about forcing recognition of the blood-stained government by the United States. p. 323

But there were soon domestic rumblings of discontent. Huerta soon found himself challenged from within by the governor of the state of Coahuila, Venustiano Carranza, who sought to restore the Mexican Constitution of 1857. Wile no fan of Madero, he correctly saw that Huerta was going to undo all of the gains made since 1910. Carranza shrewdly chose the name 'Constitutionalists" for his forces.

In addition, he took the title not of provisional president, but of First Chief. Carranza appeared to Wilson as the "governmental" type with which he could work. The British support helped Huerta to keep Carranza at bay, but Wilson soon made good on his promise to unseat Huerta. At first, the approach take by Wilson was diplomatic. Only later would he resort to force, unwillingly, to unseat Huerta. Wilson seemed to view Mexico a project where he could bring democracy to flow forth if he could just control the conditions in Mexico.

First Wilson talked the British out of supporting Huerta by promising them the protection of foreign interests in the event of a Constitutionalist victory. Wilson made one small error, in that he did not consult with Carranza before making promises in his name. To achieve his goal, Wilson was now forced to bring Carranza into the deal after the fact, giving Carranza political advantage for later diplomatic discussions.

Wilson first offered to send American troops to help overthrow Huerta, which Carranza quickly and wisely rejected. Carranza was no fool, and he knew he could not come to power as a puppet of Washington. To rule, his victory would have to be domestic, won with Mexican blood. Wilson was stuck, and to get Carranza's assent to the British deal, Wilson had to lift the American arms embargo on Mexico.

Wilson also found the opportunity to militarily confront Huerta on the flimsiest of pretexts. After a small confrontation in which the US sailors were arrested11 in the Mexican port of Tampico. They were jailed because they were in a restricted part of town. The Mexican commander however, quickly cleared the issue up and the sailors were released with a verbal apology. Had it been during Taft's administration, it would seem that little more would have been said of the situation.

The US commander on the scene, Admiral Mayo, demanded an apology; the court-martialing of the arresting Mexican officer and official salute (in the form of a 21-gun salute) before American honor would be satisfied. Anything less would be grounds for action on the part of the United States. Mayo did this on his own volition, and gained approval only after the fact.

When the salute was not forth coming, US forces invaded and occupied Vera Cruz for a period of almost a year. The battle and occupation cost the United States 19 Americans killed and 71 wounded. On the Mexican side, it cost the lives of hundreds of Mexican civilians. (Schmitt p. 139)

To give a size of the scale of the battle, 55 Medals of Honor were issued in connection with the action at Veracruz. The battle proved to be much larger than Wilson expected, who did not really think that the Mexicans would resist him, since he was bringing good government to Mexico. Writes Schmitt,

> Having maneuvered himself into the occupation of Vera Cruz by a combination of personal stubbornness over a trivial incident, of more self-righteousness about a dictator, and of a misunderstanding of Mexican nationalist attitudes, Wilson found himself tangled in a web that he did not know how to break out of. Not only was he appalled and unnerved when he learned of the extent of the fighting and the casualties, but he was disheartened by accusations of imperialism and interventionism (Schmitt p. 138)

The occupation of Vera Cruz weakened Huerta in two ways. The first was the shame of being unable to push American forces off of Mexican soil. Secondly, and more important, it denied Huerta the revenue from the Vera Cruz Customs House, a major source of income for Huerta's regime. By August of 1914, Huerta would be driven from power, with Carranza taking control in Mexico City.

While Wilson's plan succeeded in removing Huerta, it almost failed. The invasion of Vera Cruz provided Huerta with an external threat around which the Mexican people could rally. Had Wilson ordered American troops to advance onto Mexico City, ala Scott, there seems little question that Carranza, Villa, Zapata and all the other opposition leaders would have rallied to the Mexican flag in order to resist the American invaders.

Carranza, like Madero, faced a threat from Villa and Zapata, who were his erstwhile allies. As soon as Carranza gained power, he had to worry about others challenging his position. For a short time, Zapata and Villa managed to take from Mexico City, but he soon retook it. Zapata's concerns did not extend beyond Southern Mexico.

Zapata wanted fair treatment for his people and a radical distribution of land. He did not want to control the reigns of power in Mexico City. Villa also lacked the capacity or the desire to truly run Mexico. It seemed that Villa was happier with controlling Northern Mexico than with running the entire nation. Villa was never able to make the transition from rebel to statesman, with his ambition outstripping his skill at statecraft.

In April of 1915, Carranza's forces, led by General Alvaro Obregon, defeated Villa forces at Celaya. It is work noting that Obregon was helped in his victory by the tutelage of staff officers of the Kaiser's Imperial Army, who were sent to help the Mexicans.

Obregon has the benefit of German experiences on the Western Front, and from that point on, Villa ceased to be a direct military threat to Carranza. While Villa would at times challenge Carranza's position, he would never again have the military force that he had at Celaya.

By 1915, Obregon was considered by many people the true power behind the throne in revolutionary Mexico. Through his military leadership, Obregon gave Carranza the time to build a functioning government. Lesley Byrd Simpson writes that Obregon was "the real leader of the Revolution" (Simpson p. 30) Carranza consolidated power, and by October of 1915, Wilson offered Carranza de facto recognition.

Carranza asked that Wilson stop supplying Villa with arms, to which Wilson complied. Wilson had for a short time toyed with the idea of backing Villa, but over time moved towards Carranza as a more suitable (and perhaps stable) leader for Mexico.

In March of 1916, perhaps upset at the loss of American support, or just desperate to be a player in Mexican politics, Villa launched an attack on the town of Columbus, New Mexico. 18 people were killed and town center was burned to the ground. The attack provoked a firestorm of protest in the United States, and Wilson sent General Blackjack Pershing in "hot pursuit" of Villa.

What was to ensure was an eleven month long incursion by US troops hundred of miles into the Mexican state of Chihuahua. While a military failure, it did provide the US Army with much needed field experience, and a chance to develop the staff skills needed to run and support a large army in Europe.

American and Constitutionalist forces tired to avoid each other, and American forces were forbidden to enter any towns. What occurred was not peace and was not war. Carranza at first simply wanted to contain the penetration of American forces, and then get them out Mexico as fast as possible. Pershing wanted only to capture Villa and cared little for a military confrontation with Constitutionalist forces.

The Mexicans demanded that the Americans leave, and then they could jointly resolve the problem of cross border raids. The United States countered by offering to work out a plan after they captured Villa. Both sides tired avoided open confrontation, but the political strain started to show.

To resolve this impasse, both sides formed the Joint Commission to find a solution. The Commission met in New London, CT between September 1916 and January 1917. While the commission met numerous times, it never reached an accord. The Expedition would end only when Woodrow Wilson chooses to end the expedition unilaterally. The one sticking point was whether the United States would withdraw before or after an accord was reached on dealing with border raids.

Militarily, Constitutionalist and American forces did clashed twice, in the towns of Parral and Carrizal. While there were some losses, (at Carrizal, both sides suffered 25% casualties) commanders on both sides moved to keep the conflict from escalating. This could have quickly escalated into a full war, but that was something that neither Wilson or Carranza wanted or could easily afford.

Others however, did favor an open war. Both Senator Albert Fall of New Mexico and General Obregon, who had defeated Villa, wanted to fight a war, but calmer heads prevailed. Many on both sides wanted to resolve the tensions between the United States and Mexico once and for all, be it by force or diplomacy.

Had the war in Europe not been a concern in back of the minds of many Americans, the restraint on American action in Mexico may have been insufficient to prevent a full-scale war. Many tend to look back on the American contribution to the Allied War effort in Europe and conclude that a war with Mexico would have been easy. This analysis is flawed however.

First, this fails to take into account that much of the weapons used by the United States, such as aircraft, were provided by our Allies, such as France and England. It also overlooks the fact that it took General Pershing the better part of a year to prepare for combat on the Western Front, and to sufficiently trained troops for combat.

Second, a defeat of Mexico would by no means be assured, and one could question how much support such a war would have in the United States. It is important to remember that Villa acted alone and the head of a band of rebels, not as a representative of the Mexican government. The people of Mexico could be expected to vigorously defend themselves from an invasion from the North.

In January of 1917, Wilson saw that the threat from Germany was greater than the threat posed by Mexico and he order Pershing to return with his command to the United States. The "hot pursuit" never came close to catching Villa, and it served only to degrade an already strained relationship between the United States and Mexico.

Concerns over events in Mexico were to move from strategic to judicial, as a Mexican constitutional convention met in the city of Queretaro in November of 1916. By January of 1917 they had a constitution ready for Carranza to promulgate it, which he did on February 5, 1917.

CHAPTER FIVE

▼

THE MEXICAN CONSTITUTION OF 1917

The Mexican Constitution of 1917 was to a major point of conflict between the United States and Mexico during this period. The Constitution of 1917 was quite complex, encompassing 136 primary and 16 transitory articles. The constitution is one of the most sweeping and socially advanced documents in effect today. In 1917, it was considered quite radical, and was to invoke concerns not only in the United States, but also in Europe, especially England. Writes historian w. Dirk Ratt,

> In all, it was a federalist, anticlerical, nationalist document that subordinated individual property rights to the Mexican nation and, if put into effect, would repudiate the established rule of international intercourse and Wilson's idea of free enterprise. (Ratt p. 115)

For the United Sates, the most important article, and the one that would cloud relations throughout the 1920s was Article 27. It was this one article that was to cause great concern in the United States and was to lead for calls of intervention in some quarters of the American government. Article 27 represented a dramatic revision of the economic and political relationship between the United States and Mexico.

Villa may have been a threat to public safety along the border, but this was a threat to large American investments in Mexico. The article also represented a threat to the capitalist system and the idea of private property. More than any other event in this period, the status of Article 27 would be the crux of the cross-border relationship.

Article 27 by itself is half as long as the entire us Constitution. The Mexican Constitution reflects an attempt to redraw the blueprint of society and right what were seen as historical wrongs. The preamble of Article 27 states that

> The ownership of lands and waters comprised within the limits of the national territory is vested originally in the Nation, which has had, and has, the right to transmit title thereof to private persons, thus constituting private property. (Foreign Affairs, 1917 p. 955)

While the preamble caused some concern, it was section 1 of Article 27 that caused the most concern for American (and other foreign) companies owning property in Mexico. The stability that they had enjoyed under the Diaz regime was now threatened by a new political order. Worse, they had very little voice in this new political system, and turned to the United States to voice their concerns. The influence enjoyed over Diaz was not to be found in Revolutionary Mexico.

The greatest concern was over ownership of the oil fields, now desperately needed for the growing Allied war effort. Any action, by Mexico or Germany, that threatened the free flow of oil for the war effort was to be stopped by whatever means necessary.

Section 1 of Article 27 states that,

> Only Mexicans by birth or naturalization and Mexican compa-
> nies have the right to acquire ownership in lands, waters and the
> appurtenances, or to obtain concessions to develop mines,
> waters or mineral fuels in the Republic of Mexico. The nation
> may grant the same right to foreigners, provided they agree
> before the Department of Foreign Affairs to be considered
> Mexicans in respect to such property, and accordingly not to
> invoke the protection of their government in respect to the same,
> under penalty, in case of breech, of forfeiture to the Nation of
> property so acquired. Within a zone of 100 kilometers from the
> frontier, and 50 kilometers from the seacoast, no foreigner shall
> under any condition acquire direct ownership of lands and
> waters. (Foreign Affairs, 1917, p. 955)

There were two elements that were an anathema in the United States.
First, the loss of the protection of the government was of great importance
to the American companies, as they would have no recourse if events
turned hostile with Mexico. American businessmen who invested in foreign countries had traditionally enjoyed this "big stick" protection that
came with being "an American" citizen.

If Mexico decided to nationalize the oil industry, they could complain
only to their new government, the Mexican government. They could not
turn to a sympathetic ear in Washington, which could bring diplomatic,
economic and military pressure to bear. American interests in other countries had always counted on turning to the threat of action by the United
States to reinforce their position.

If they were forced to become Mexican citizens, that complaint, naturally,
would fall on deaf and uncaring ears. The drafter's of the Mexican
Constitution still had the Punitive Expedition fresh in their memory, and
wished to avoid, at all costs, the invocation of American force. By making

foreign investors Mexican citizens, they felt they could prevent any outside action against Mexican domestic policy.

It was the final sentence however, that caused the most concern for Washington. This ban on foreign ownership along the border had clear implications for the United States. All of the oil and most of the mining in Mexico fell within this exclusion zone.

They would either have to choose Mexican citizenship, which eliminated the protection of the American government, or they would have to give up their very substantial investments at almost a total loss, since they could sell their holdings to no one but Mexicans. In 1918, American capital investment in the oil sector of the Mexican economy alone amounted to $ 200,000,000.00 (Meyer Oil Controversy p. 10)

It is the unique nature of the Mexican Constitution that amendments do not carry the force of law. In the United States, the ratification of an amendment is sufficient for it to be considered to have the force of law. Since the first Amendment of the United States Constitution states that, "Congress shall make no law respecting an establishment of religion..." this is considered to have the force of law.

In contrast, the amendments of the Mexican Constitution are considered statements of intent, and require the passage of enabling legislation. Even though the Mexican Constitution was ratified in 1917, it could be years before the Mexican Congress passed the legislation necessary to give it the force of law.

The period between the ratification of the Constitution and the passage of enabling legislation gave these companies time to plan a strategy for lobbying, both in Mexico and the United States. While cornered, American investors could bring great forces to bear in an attempt to protect their economic and political interests in Mexico.

The debate over Article 27 hinged on two crucial points. The first was whether Article 27 would ever be enforced by Mexican government. The second was if Article 27 was put into force, would it be applied retroactively, or from the date of enforcement. This was an important point, since American companies had continued to drill and explore after February 7, 1917. If Article 27 was made retroactive to the date of ratification, it would impact projects that foreign governments had ongoing.

The conflict over Article 27 was to last six years, until Mexico and the United States reached accord on the issue under the Bucareli Agreement of 1923. Indeed, even then the issue was resolved not through formal treaty, but a series of agreements and accords that put off the final resolution until a much later date.

CHAPTER SIX

▼

MEXICO'S NEUTRALITY IN WORD WAR ONE

A concurrent concern for the United Sates was Mexico's supposed neutrality in 1917-1918. With the American entrance in to World war One, there was a great deal of American apprehension over Mexico's relationship with Imperial Germany. The relationship between Mexico and Germany was seen as a threat to American security and to the Allied war effort. People were quick to point out that it was the Ypiranga, a German ship, that was bringing arms and ammunition to Vera Cruz in 1914, and it was the Ypiranga that carried Diaz into comfortable exile in Europe.

Carranza was known to have pro-German leanings, and allowed German military advisors to assist Obregon in the defeat of villa at the battle of Celaya in 1915. Writes John S.D. Eisenhower,

> The introduction of barbed wire and machine guns on large scale made frontal attacks on entrenched positions suicidal.

Obregon had learned about these techniques from a German advisor, Colonel Maximilian Kloss. (Eisenhower p. 176)

Carranza made much of the neutrality of Mexico, and tried to keep Mexico from being drawn into the war with the United States. In addition, Carranza saw Mexican neutrality as a means of both rejecting American influence and bringing Mexico back into the world arena. The Kaiser had recognized Carranza's government in 1916.

A number of German officers joined Carranza army as advisors for his fights against the various rebel factions. Carranza's interpretation of neutrality was to get him into trouble more than once in the international community.

Carranza's attitude towards German was shared by others in Mexico, especially the Army. This attitude was a response, in part, as what could be seen as American attempts at interference. Writes Douglas Richmond,

> While the government was split over which side to support during World War One, the army favored Carranza's tilt toward Germany. Typical of the army's pro-German stance was Jacinto B. Trevino's order to General Francisco Gonzalez to drop his "reactionary" pro-Allied friends. Gonzalez, in an outburst of anger at being overcharged by a German padlock firm, had insulted the German consul. Germans however, did enjoy some degree of popularity, (Richmond p. 155-156)

This pro-German attitude was also seen in other parts of Mexican society, especially the Mexican business community. German enjoyed a growing trade with Mexico before the war, and the positive image of the German carried through the war. Writes Richmond,

> Pro-German sentiment was also strong within commercial circles and the army. Partially as a result of German influence during the late Porfiriato, Mexican businesses often utilized German

products. Traditionally, terms of trade with Germany were much fairer than with other major powers. Germans bought mines and property abandoned during the Revolution, while Berlin no longer protested Carranza's banking laws. (Richmond p. 203)

On February 6, 1917, Carranza offered official best wishes to the Kaiser, coming only eight days after the Germans notified the United States that it was resuming unrestricted submarine warfare. The New York Times reported that "General Carranza has set his best wishes to the German Emperor" (NYT 2/7/1917 p. 22).

The announcement caused something of an uproar on the international scene, and Carranza was forced to issue an explanation through the Mexican Foreign Office. The clarification stated that it

"Officially denied that Carranza had telegraphed his congratulation to the German Emperor on the international situation, explaining that Carranza had sent felicitations on the Emperor's birthday" (NYT 2/8/17 p. 22)

Less than a week later, Carranza would add grist to the mill about his pro-German leanings when he issued a most unusual call to the other neutral nations in World War One. Carranza invited other nations to "join with Mexico in an international agreement to prohibit the exportation of munitions to the belligerent in Europe" (NYT 2/14/1917 p. 1) In essence, Carranza was proposing a massive rewriting of the accepted standards of trade by neutrals.

While the offer may have seemed to be neutral in nature, it in fact greatly favored the Central Powers. By 1917, the Allies were heavily dependant on American supplies, especially oil and foodstuff products. Germany's surface navy had been inactive since Jutland.

More importantly, Germany lacked the merchant fleet with which to import war material. If the Germans had a blockade on England, then the

English had a far more effective one on Germany. To stop neutral trade with the belligerents would serve to only strengthen Germany's hand.

Like the birthday wishes for the Kaiser, Carranza's "neutrality offer" had few supporters in the United States. Wrote the New York Times,

> This proposal, contrary to international law and to the principles of neutrality as laid down by the United States in its notes to the German and Austro-Hungarian Governments, caused critics of international affairs to say that as the Central Powers were the only ones to be benefited by the proposal, it was probably due to German influence on....Carranza or Carranza's own desire to have a hand in the European quarrel. (NYT 2/14/17 p.1)

In its editorial of the same day, the New York Times wrote in a piece titled Carranza's New Freak that

> "It must be taken as fresh and convincing evidence of active and persistent German intrigue in Mexico." (NYT 2/14/17 p. 8)

The proposal was quickly and resoundingly rejected by the United States, and the offer would fade to the background until March of 1917, when the existence of the infamous Zimmerman telegram was made public by Woodrow Wilson.

▼

CHAPTER SEVEN

THE ZIMMERMAN TELEGRAM

On January 16, 1917, the German Foreign Minister, Arthur Zimmerman, sent a telegram to Count Johann Von Bernstorff, the German Ambassador to the United States. In this telegram, Von Bernstorff was given the task of forwarding the message to Heinrich Von Eckhardt, the German Minister to Mexico. This telegram was to be one of the two catalysts that were to propel the United Sates into World War One.

In the telegram, the Mexican government was to be informed by Von Eckhardt that Germany was resuming unrestricted submarine warfare on February 1, 1917, and that furthermore, German wished to invite Mexico to make common cause with the Central Powers. In return, Mexico, on the conclusion of an anticipated German victory, would be given the lost territories of New Mexico, Texas and Arizona, and would receive generous financial aid to fund such an effort.

The Zimmerman telegram became a cause celebre not only for its content, but also for how the United States found out about it. The British, and the start of the war, had cut Germany's only transatlantic cable. There after, German was forced to use a radio to send out all messages, governmental, diplomatic and military.

The British government had been intercepting and decoding these documents, and when they started to decode the Zimmermann telegram, they soon realized that they had bonanza on their hands. The British were quite shrewd, as they did not immediately share the information with the United States, but rather waited for the most opportune time to 'release' the telegram.

In late February of 1917, without fully revealing the source of the telegram, the British gave the telegram to the United States. After consideration of the importance of the telegram, Wilson made the information public on March 1, 1917, and there was an immediate firestorm of protest. On March 2, the day after the existence of the telegram was revealed, the New York Times wrote

> The intercepted (Zimmerman) telegram was dated Jan. 19. CARRANZA's disingenuous note the neutral powers, proposing a joint prohibition of all supplies to the belligerent countries in Europe, was dated Feb 12. In the light of the new revelation, it reads like a reply to Germany (NYT 3/2/17 p. 10)

The Zimmerman telegram was seen by many as a conformation of German intrigues in Mexico. On March 15, it was reported that "Neutral Diplomat Discloses Kaiser's Apparent Grip on the Republic." The article went on to state that

> "confidential sources state...the German Bank in Mexico and German Legation there are guiding virtually the entire financial and diplomatic affairs of Mexico" (NYT 3/15/17 p. 1)

The telegram was met with scorn and concern. Scorn that few considered Mexico much of a military threat, and concern that while Mexico could not hope in defeating the United States, it could tie up vast amounts of resources in the Southwest, rather than being employed in Europe. Wrote the New Republic,

> To offer the almost bankrupt Carranza government, whose army consisted of a few thousand ill equipped and ill trained peons as payment for Mexican assistance against the United States, three sovereign American states, whose able bodied men, if properly armed, could easily overrun the whole of Mexico-diplomacy of this kind is saved from being monstrous chiefly by being so utterly absurd. (New Republic 3/1/17 p. 151-152)

There was concern however; that a Mexico allied with Germany could cause problems with the Allied war effort. By 1917, the British fleet was getting 75% of its fuel from Mexico. (Meyers Oil Controversy p. 67) Mexican oil was considered vital war material, and the Allies would not allow the oil to be cut of, or worse, used for the German cause. The Allies worried about German submarine bases in Mexico, and idea put forth by Carranza in 1916.

Carranza, while he may have flirted with the idea of a German-Mexican alliance, knew that the United States would do what was necessary to achieve his war aims. While he could peruse his novel policy of "strict neutrality", Carranza was aware of just how far he could push the United States.

In 1916, Carranza had lacked the strength to effectively challenge the American incursion into Mexico after Villa, and he knew that as American geared up for war with Germany, Mexico would stand little chance of facing down a strengthened America. Wisely, Carranza used the period from 1917-1918 to consolidate his position while the United States was occupied by the war in Europe. Carranza was sitting on the sidelines to see how the German cause went in 1918.

While Wilson's attention may have been diverted overseas, the American public still paid attention to what was going on in Mexico. The majority of the concern centered on the actions of Carranza and of the real and perceived threat of Germans influence in and on Mexico. Wrote the Outlook Magazine in late March of 1917,

> The German menace in Mexico is, in fact, much more serious than that of a mere political threat. Under the new Mexican Constitution....Carranza, might, with apparent consistency, lease every oil well in Mexico to German operators on the grounds that British, Dutch and American concessions are nullified. (Outlook 3/21/17 p. 498)

The same theme is seen in other works of the period. The New York Times, as stated earlier, editorialized on both Carranza's "neutrality proposal" and the birthday wishes for the Kaiser, both in 1917 and 1918. The telegram was clear evidence of favoritism towards the Germans and a direct threat to the United States.

In October of 1918, the Century magazine editorialized on the situation in Mexico and the influence of Mexico. The article, reflecting the strong anti-German feelings of the war years, states that,

> As for Mexico, that, as always, is an unpleasant subject. Mexico may be neutral in name; in fact it is pro-German to an extreme. The land of Montezuma is not an important country in the same sense as the progressive ABC (Argentina, Brazil and Chile) nations. It is important to the United States in somewhat the same way that a hospital for contagious diseases would become important to you if it should move next door to your house. (10/10/18 p. 12)

Mexico has long been infested with all sorts of social germs, from peaceful graft to murderous revolution, and now it has the Teutonic bacillus. If proof were needed, it would be sufficient to call to mind the proposal of President Carranza, made in February of last year, that all countries of this hemisphere should be what pro- Germans call "genuine neutrals"; in other words, should stop exporting anything to any of the belligerents

In the magazine The World's Work, a November 1918 article entitled German efforts in Mexico detailed German actions in Mexico. These articles reflect a fear of not only the presence of Germans in Mexico, but of a fear of their influence on the Mexico government. From running the government to training the Mexican Army, there was widespread fear of the influence of the Germans in Mexico. As always, the underlying fear was being cut from access to oil. In addition, an Army trained by the Germans was not something that the United States wanted its border. Raiding bandits was one thing, but a Mexican Army with German arms and tactics was another. In the article from The World's Work, the concern is over the penetration of the key elements of the Mexican army. The article states that,

> The serious and professional part of the otherwise happy-go-lucky picnic called the Mexican army has been obsessed by German military efficiency, in theory and in practice. They have made good use of German reservists in the more scientific parts of their army organization. In addition to German employees in the Government wireless plants, German and Japanese are showing Mexicans how to manufacture ammunition, and other Germans are employed in the aviation plant where Carranza's favorite nephew, young Colonel Salinas, is superintending in Mexico City. (World's Work 11/18 p. 6)

Forty German officers hold commissions in the politico-military Constitutionalist army.

Research has shown that there was some foundation for American fears of a German presence in Mexico. From oil to strategic materials, unfettered access to Mexican resources was vital to the Allied war effort, and the United States could not brook any interference from anyone.

Secretary of State Lansing, fearing the pro-German attitude of Carranza's government left the United States with little choice but to act preemptively, suggesting that the United States occupy the entire oil producing regions of Mexico, take over the Tehuantepec railroad and deploy troops along the border. (Meyer p. 45) Wilson resisted, and the plan came to nothing.

That Lansing would consider such a plan however, does give an indication as how serious the Allies viewed unfettered access to Mexican resources, especially oil. Anything that interrupted this access had to be prevented, regardless of cost. Within all of the fears, there was some foundation for concern. Writes Gilderhus in his work Diplomacy and Revolution,

> More reliable evidence suggested that Germans intended sabotage in the oil fields, that wireless stations tried to aid German submarines in attacking American shipping, and that German propagandist preyed upon Mexican antipathies towards the United States. (Gilderhus p. 65)

Carranza did little to dispel concerns over his pro-German leanings. He tried to distance himself from the telegram, but he did not openly renounce the Zimmermann offer. It is worthy to note that the offer in the Zimmermann telegram also included Japan. But Japan refused the offer to obtain the best diplomatic position.

She quickly denounced the Zimmermann telegram and later declared war on the Central powers (and thus gaining German territory in the Pacific that would be the scene of major battles in World War Two) and becoming one of the allied powers, even sending Japanese destroyers to patrol in the Mediterranean Sea. By towing the Allied line, the Japanese were able to make great gains in Asia from very small diplomatic and military investments.

While Carranza was able to maintain Mexican independence in the face of American demands, it would not come without a price. In early 1917, Mexican officials approached JP Morgan to try and secure a $ 10,000,000.00 loan to help rebuild a shattered Mexico. Morgan would not consider the request. A Carranza request to lift an arms embargo was not even forwarded to Wilson for consideration.

Only after Carranza reassured Washington that Article 27 was not to be confiscatory did relations start to return to a normal state. Mexico publicly announced that it was going to try and seek a loan from the United States. Carranza was in many ways pragmatic, and was willing to do what was necessary to sustain Mexico.

This served to reassure Wilson that Carranza was moving away from his flirtation with Germany. On August 20, 1917, Wilson said that he would not be "morally" opposed to American loans to Mexico, and on August 31, 1917 Wilson moved Carranza from de facto to de jure recognition.

With this recognition came a lifting of the arms embargo a fortnight later. But Carranza was unable to secure a loan, and his position in Mexico was becoming increasingly untenable, as debt mounted and Mexico lacked the funds to rebuild after years of revolution.

Carranza was facing repeated eruptions of rebellion, which we placing a great drain on the few resources that he had available. To compound matters, Carranza faced the threat of many whom wished to challenge him for the 1920 election.

The most immediate threat to Carranza was that he was running out of money. By 1917, the army was consuming 60% of his monthly expenditures. His government was taking in 11 million pesos a month, but was spending 16.5 million in outlays. (Bethell p. 178)

Mexico was at a crossroads, as Carranza tried to find a way to implement the new Constitution and find a way to generate enough revenue to get the government back on its feet, and to solidify his own position in Mexico.

Without loans from the United States or elsewhere, Mexico would be stuck in her shattered state. More importantly, Mexico had not made payments on her existing debt, and this made getting funding all that more difficult. The only area of the Mexican economy that was generating anything resembling revenue was the oil sector, and it was to here that Carranza turned to generate revenue.

Chapter Eight

▼

1918 War and Oil

By 1918 Carranza found himself backed into a corner. On February 18, 1918, Carranza took a step that was a mixture of desperation and nerve. As part of Article 27, Carranza decreed that a new tax would be levied on the oil industry. As a first step towards compliance with the tax decree, Carranza set a May 20th deadline for the registrations of oil land titles. This registration would open up the denouncement of all lands that were not registered. The tax would not only apply to oil that was produced, but also to rents and royalties that were paid in conjunction of the production of oil. Writes Linda Hall,

> Carranza reiterated the nation's right to all oil deposits; asserted that all those wishing to exploit such rights must apply to the government for permission; and indicated that in the event of noncompliance, the landholder or company involved would lose its right and third parties could claim the land in question after a certain date. In effect, Carranza was declaring that land titles

granted to oil companies by earlier governments were actually
only temporary concessions (Hill p. 104)

This move had an immediate impact on Carranza's foreign relations
with the United States, which was quick to denounce the oil tax a confiscatory. This was not the first tax placed on oil by Carranza. In early 1917,
Carranza had put forth a simple tax on the oil industry in order to raise
revenues for the treasury. Oil companies had paid that tax, albeit under
protest. This tax was different for two reasons however. First, it was much
broader, as it was levied not only on production but also on rents and royalties. Secondly, it also pushed the idea of registering titles; the oil companies saw this as the first step towards complete confiscation of American
holdings in Mexico.

When the deadline of May 20th arrived, Mexico was in no position to
impose the new tax decree, so Carranza moved the deadline to July 31, 1918,
and then moving it to August 15th. In that period, Carranza waited for the
outcome of the latest (and final) German push of the war. The German
attack across the Marne started on July 16th, and by the second week of
August it was clear that German was not going to break the Allied lines.

When it became clear that the fortunes of war had turned against the
Germans, Carranza dropped the requirement that the oil companies register their titles, thus reducing the tax decree to a simple tax. As a further
sign of his weak position, Carranza instructed his Minister of Finance,
Alberto Pani, to being talks with the United States in order to create a
mutually acceptable law that would place Article 27 into force.

The end of World War was to spell the end of Carranza's attempt to
play the United States off Germany. With the signing of the armistice, the
United States was left as the only foreign power that could exercise decisive influence over Mexico.

Its greatest weapon, recognition of Carranza, could be used as a carrot
or a stick, as the situation warranted, forcing the American position on the
issue of Article 27. Germany could not intervene, and Britain was too

beholden (and indebted) to the United States to protest anything the she might do in regards to Mexico. Writes Knight,

> Europe, prostrate, could not contest American policy in the Western Hemisphere during the oil disputes of the 1920s Great Britain tended lamely to follow the American lead. The United States now espoused a new, albeit vague, project of hemisphere free trade (a modest precursor of the global project of 1945). Government was more committed to sustaining American businesses overseas in the uncertain postwar world. (Knight p. 126)

It is perhaps telling of the American character that Mexico was not invaded in 1918, as there was no force that could possibly oppose her. Self-restraint, not the threat of opposing force, stayed the American hand. Short of concern about world opinion, the United States could have rolled across Mexico with little effort. That we did not speaks something about the American character.

With the end of the war came the Spanish Influenza, which ravaged across Mexico, killing more than 400,000 people. The pandemic was to strike hardest at those between 20 and 40, so that in only four months, 4% of the able bodied Mexicans died. (Bethel p. 185) For a country weakened by war and strife, the influenza pandemic was simply one more barrier to an effective political and economic recovery. In a cruel twist of fate, the areas hardest hit by the influenza were the same areas that suffered the most from the Revolution.

CHAPTER NINE

▼

1919-STORM CLOUDS

The year 1919 was to prove a decisive one for Mexican-US relations. It was to be the last year that invasion was a very real fear and possibility for the Mexicans. 1919 would also be a period of slow but steady erosion of the power that Carranza had tried to build for himself in the preceding three years.

By the beginning of 1921-22, the United States had chosen to use political engagement (using the granting and withdrawal of recognition as an inducement) rather than military force to resolve differences between the two sides. This change in policy would follow closely the change in approach between the Wilson administration and the Harding administration, as confrontation gave way to engagement.

This engagement would follow a hazardous path, but came to fruition for the United States with the signing of the Bucareli Agreements in 1923. The United States would learn by 1923 to work with the administration in Mexico City, rather than resort to the threat of naked force and intervention. Until that time however, the United States and Mexico still had to resolve some core differences between them.

The American Yearbook-1919 summed up the situation between the two nations succinctly, writing that,

> "Relations between Mexico and the United States during the year were characterized by diplomatic crisis' that brought forth caustic notes and rejoinders from the capitals of both countries." (American Yearbook p. 120)

The Annual Register, the English version of the American yearbook, echoed these sentiments concerning the poor relations between the two nations, writing,

> "The best that can be said of conditions in this troubled republic [Mexico] during the year is that they did not grow any worse. "(Annual Register p. 288)

The development of relations between 1919-1923 was the first step towards what would become known in the 1930's as the Good Neighbor Policy. The heavy-handed and one-sided approach of Henry Lane Wilson was gradually but firmly being replaced with a more interactive method of engagement when the position of the other side was actually considered before taking action. The failures of Vera Cruz and the villa Expedition had given pause to those who advocated military action. While there would always be Albert Fall's demanding intervention, most would opt for diplomatic engagement and the seeking of common ground. According to David Bailey,

> [A]lthough Washington had often been vexed by the behavior of the Mexican regimes, it had come to believe that it could probably live with them. The Bucareli agreements of 1923 had indicated

that the revolutionary leadership could be reasonable and that diplomacy could defend American interests. Moreover, experience had shown that trouble between the two countries came when central authority was weak in Mexico. {Bailey p. 307)

Mexican Trade with the United States

For all the diplomatic conflict between 1916-1919, trade was still taking place between the two nations. Not only was the trade in oil increasing, but during this period of trade in other commodities also rose dramatically. These items include such products as cattle hide, copper, coffee, cotton and sisal.

This trade was crucial to Mexico, since it provided one of the few sources of income for a country that had yet to rebuild from the strife of the past ten years. The levels changed from year to year, depending on crops and local unrest. But the general trend was towards growing trade between the two countries. As bad as things got, and at times they were quite tense, Mexico and the United States never stopped trading with one another.

The overall trend however, is show in the graph on the next page. That the general trend was for increased trade between the two nations. Whatever the difference between the two nations, there was never a complete break of trade between the two nations.

The problem between the two nations still stemmed from when {and how) Article 27 was to be framed in its final form. While the United States felt it had great advantage over Mexico, it was still in many ways dependent on Mexico. But whatever the difference, it did not preclude trade between the two nations.

In 1919, the United States was consuming the majority of the world's oil, and there was a very real fear in the period that the world's oil supply was facing exhaustion. At the time, Mexico had one of the largest reserves known to man. Mexican oil therefore, was seen as vitally necessary for both America's growing industry and the maintenance of American defense.

During this period, America's naval fleet had made the technological transition from coal to oil fired boilers, and oil was needed in great quantities just for peacetime operations. Oil, already an economic interest of the United States, also became a strategic interest that warranted defense.

> Starting in 1919, the War Department started to draw up contingency plans that would be used against Mexico if American access to Mexican oil was threatened. The military drew a series of plans for many countries. They went under the broad heading of Rainbow plans, with each nation being assigned their own color. These military orders for Mexico were known as Special Plan Green. They would be in force until 1941 and would reach 8 inches in thickness, an indication of the amount of effort put into its planning. (Cockcroft p. 94)

The first incident, and that one that was to effect relations for the rest of the year, harkened back to Article 27. In the beginning of 1919, the Mexican Congress had authorized Carranza to use the army in order to enforce his decrees under Article 27. The oil companies were no longer free to drill, as they would have to request permission from Mexican authorities before drilling any new sites. If they did not comply with the new rules, they would face the risk of the Mexican Army coming in and shutting down their wells and refineries.

When the companies started drilling, the Mexican army was sent in and capped the new wells. The Untied States protested, seeing this as the implementation of Article 27, and the use of force against American owned property.

While the United States protested, the Mexicans prepared for an invasion that they knew they could not resist. In 1919, more than three years after the Pershing expedition, the United States and Mexico moved closer to war, and tensions rose. The core issue was still the oil industry, and how the two sides perceived Mexico's right to exploit her own resources. As always, the Mexicans saw this as an issue of national sovereignty, while the United States simply deemed it a case of protecting both her citizens and her investments overseas.

In 1919, another divisive issue was brought to the surface, the Monroe Doctrine. At the Versailles Peace Conference in 1919, the Monroe Doctrine was being discussion with an eye towards a European recognition of its validity as a policy. While the United States saw the doctrine as a means of protecting the independence of the Latin American nations, it was seen my many in Latin America as an excuse for United States intervention in the Western Hemisphere to further the goals of those in Washington. Writes John Crow in the Epic of Latin America,

> When the peoples of Latin America began their struggle for independence they found their strongest inspiration in the North America Revolution…[W]ithin a period of less than a century that almost boundless admiration turned to resentment and bitter hate. This change in sentiment marks one of the unhappiest chapters in the history of the American hemisphere. It was no sudden about-face, but the gradual result of many years of increasing tension in inter-American relations. To most Latin Americans the whole unpleasant story is summarized in the words "Monroe Doctrine" (Crow p. 675)

Mexico was not thrilled with the idea that the Monroe Doctrine would receive some formal recognition (which it did at Versailles) by the signatories of the Versailles Treaty. It was bad enough that the United States believed in the Monroe Doctrine. To give the European stamp of approval only made things worse In a note to the American government, Carranza stated that,

> The Mexican Government has learned that the recognition of the Monroe Doctrine has been under discussion at the conference in

Paris. The Mexican Government has not recognized nor will it recognize that doctrine, nor any other which attacks the sovereignty and independence of Mexico (Foreign Relations 1919 p. 545)

These tensions were to last throughout the year as both sides sought someway to bring about resolution to the problem. As had been since 1917, the differences of opinion centered on Article 27 and how it was to be implemented. Carranza had gained some breathing room with the entry of the United States into World War I, but now had few allies to which he could turn to as the United States could now focus on Mexico. In a speech given to the Mexican National Assembly in September of 1919, Carranza spoke of relations with the United States,

The Government of Mexico hopes that the Republic of the North will respect the sovereignty and independence of Mexico, because to violate them on the plea of lack of guarantees for its citizens or of legislation injurious to their interest would constitute an unpardonable transgression of the principles of international law and morality, and would give proof that the greatest misfortune of a people is that of being weak {Foreign Relations 1919 p. 534)

In the United States, the end of the World War had brought new attention to the situation in Mexico. In July of 1919, Senator Albert Fall {R-NM), who had long favored intervention in Mexico, chaired a Senate committee that was to investigate the situation in Mexico.

The Fall Committee, as it was to become known, brought in pro- and anti-Carranza supporters, members of the oil industry and others to investigate the situation in Mexico. While trying to appear balanced, the Fall Committee was seen by many in both nations as pre-cursor to intervention to Mexico. Once Fall could create a bill of indictments against Mexico, the next step would be war. The Nation magazine editorialized on the appointment of Senator Fall as chairman of the committee,

The appointment of a fire-eating committee of the United States Senate to investigate conditions in Mexico, assess damages, and to demand immediate payment for all injuries inflicted upon American citizens is an event of evil omen. With Senator Fall as chairman there is about as much chance of giving Mexico a square deal as there is of giving the Kaiser a just trail in London. Both are condemned in advance of the hearing (The Nation, 8/16/1919 p. 194-195)

The general findings of the Fall Committee were used to promote the position that recognition of Carranza should be withdrawn. Others however, used the findings as basis for calling for a full-scale military intervention in Mexico. It is worth nothing that at this time 5,000 American troops (Matloff American Military History p. 65) had just been recalled from an almost year long expedition in the Murmansk-Archangel Soviet Russia.

The governor of Texas suggested that only an armed occupation of Mexico would bring a resolution to the situation. (Meyer Oil Controversy p.71) In was in this climate that many in the United States started to prepare for what they saw as the inevitable battle that was to follow. There was little concern for the outcome of a war. Given the size and ability of the United States military in 1919, the only question would be how much will the United States had to go to war with Mexico.

After more that two years of war, the United States possessed a rather formidable military force that would face little challenge from the Mexican Army. At its height, the US Army in World War I would have 3,685,458 men in 62 divisions. (Matloff p. 33) While war with Mexico would be difficult the United States had an overwhelming advantage.

Wilson's Secretary of War, Lindsey Garrison stated that the "only antidote for what was happening in Mexico was force and intervention." (Knight p. 125) Now that the United States had the ability to challenge the Mexicans, all was needed was resolve. Given support from Washington, the

US Army could put an end to the disorder in Mexico and install a government that was more sympathetic to North American interests.

The general feeling that an invasion of Mexico was imminent was reinforced by the request made by Secretary of Navy Franklin D. Roosevelt to the State Department "that advance notice be given in the event it was decided to go ahead with the invasion of Mexico" (Meyer oil Controversy p. 71) Now, to many, it was only a matter of choosing the date and time of the invasion.

The pressure for intervention was great, but by November of 1919, Wilson decided that it was not warranted. President attention to Mexico had waned as Wilson devoted all of his efforts to the Versailles Treaty and subsequent attempts to get it ratified by the Senate. Soon after deciding not to support the idea of an invasion Wilson was felled by a stroke took him out of day to day affairs. In a period still shrouded in some mystery, President Wilson had little contact with the outside world. Most contact with the president was via his wife.

The ill health of the President was to encourage Senator Fall to lead an unsuccessful campaign to have Wilson removed from office. It was to be claimed later by Josephus Daniels, once Wilson's Secretary of the Navy, that the oil interests were behind Senator Fall's active role in the attempt to remove the incapacitated Wilson from office. (Meyers oil p. 71)

During Wilson's recovery, there was an episode that was to fuel the demands for intervention in Mexico. Many felt that it was Wilson's policies that had created the situation in Mexico, and that only a firm hand could restore order in Mexico and restore respect for the United States on the part of Mexicans.

Soon after Wilson fell ill, an American counsel in Puebla, William Jenkins was kidnapped, and a ransom demanded. Fall used the situation to reiterate his demands for intervention. The Jenkins Affair, as it was known, was seen by many as the perfect pretext for revocation of recognition, and perhaps even intervention in Mexico.

The United States had the excuse it desired and the means to execute an invasion. All it needed now was the will to give the order and invade Mexico. Perhaps Wilson's legacy is not only what he did, but like Eisenhower, what he did not do. The kidnapping reinforced for many North Americans the feeling that there was a lack of respect on the part of Mexico. In addition, it was seen as a prime example of Carranza's inability to maintain order in Mexico. For those spoiling for a fight, this was pretext enough for war. Wrote the newsmagazine, The Nation,

Jenkins incidents come and go, but oil flows on forever. Behind all anti-Mexican propaganda lies one fundamental fact -Article 27 of the new Constitution, nationalizing the petroleum deposits. The present Mexican government is attempting, so far as possible, to revoke for the people the wonderful national resources granted to individuals and corporations under the old government.

In that attempt it has come into conflict with the powerful business interest, both Mexican and American, with which it ought to deal justly, as it apparently intends to do. It would be to the everlasting shame of the American people if they allow their Government to make war on Mexico on such flimsy and immoral pretexts as the Jenkins incident, joined to the scheme of the oil interests, affords. (The Nation 12/6/1917 p. 708)

The immediate crisis passed quickly however when six days later an anonymous Mexican citizen, wanting to avoid an American invasion, paid the demanded ransom. People on both sides of the border breathed a sigh of relief that the issue had not come to martial blows.

But then elements on the Mexican side made a political move that served to only anger the United States and bring about a renewed demand for intervention in Mexico, as the actions were now seen to becoming from the Mexican government, rather than uncontrollable bandits in the countryside.

Two weeks after his release, Jenkins was arrested by General Luis Gonzalez, who was the military commander in the Puebla area an aspirant to the presidency. Gonzalez charged Jenkins with staging the entire kidnapping in order to fuel American demands for intervention. Not only did this out-rage Americans; it was seen as yet another example of the lawlessness that existed throughout Mexico.

The outcry in the United States was swift and predictable. This was simply one more example of how Carranza was not fully in control of Mexico. What infuriated many Americans was that Jenkins was not just an U.S. citizen, but that he was a consular official.

The kidnappings were bad enough, but this was now a case of a Mexican official arresting an American diplomatic official. Allover again, this was seen as a national insult against the United States by a Mexico that had no respect for authority. All the insults and slights of the past nine years came cascading down into a long term rage at how the United States was treated by Mexico.

On December 3, 1919, Senator Fall introduced a resolution in the Senate calling on Wilson to sever relations with Mexico, calling Carranza's administration in Mexico City a "pretend government." (Bethel p. 190) The Mexicans reacted swiftly the next day by releasing Jenkins from custody. On December B, 1919, Wilson rejected Fall's resolution. The New York Times reported that Wilson rejected Fall suggestion, writing,

> he [Wilson] would resent any resolution on the part of the Senate because foreign relations should be handled exclusively by the executive branch of government and advice should not be tendered by the Senate unless on request from him. (NYT 12/9/19 p. 1)

The Jenkins Affair, while it lasted, was a source of great discussion in the United States. It came to represent all that was wrong with Mexico and Wilson's foreign policy. The United States had not forcefully defended its position or its honor, and now Mexico was exploiting that weakness. What was needed was firm action on the part of the United States.

Wilson's Secretary of State, Robert Lansing, fearful of the effect the Fall Committee, wrote Wilson in December of 1919, prior to Wilson's meeting with Senators Fall and Hitchcock. Lansing wrote the ill Wilson,

> I have not troubled you with the Jenkins case which is of considerable complexity as to fact and as to law because there was no possibility of that case developing a situation which could possibly warrant intervention in Mexico. As to this I am sure that the Foreign Relations Committee is in entire accord. The real Mexican situation is the whole series of outrages wrongs which Americans in Mexico have suffered during the Carranza administration....The danger is that Congress, in view of the facts which will be reported undoubtedly by Senator Fall's sub-Committee on Mexico, will demand drastic action or put us in a position where it will be very difficult to treat the matter with a proper deliberation. I have seen this coming for some time, knowing the vast amount of material collected by the Fall Committee and it was with that purpose that I sought to divert attention to the Jenkins case (Wilson Vol. 64 p. 127)

This period also gave rise to a series of proposals to effect a geo-political solution. Henry Lane Wilson, who since being removed as ambassador spent his time calling for intervention in Mexico, had a novel solution to the "Mexico" problem. The problem had always been one of security and access to oil.

Henry Lane Wilson proposed the creation of a border state that would be up of all the area between the Mexican-US border and the 22° parallel. This buffer state, to be taken by force if necessary, would contain the area from which Carranza had emerged. It would also contain a great deal if the mineral of Mexico.

The American press played up the idea of intervention in Mexico, especially in Southwest and California, were fears of Mexico ran deep, and where there were a large number of Mexican immigrants. Some of the concerns in these areas stemmed from racism, and a genuine fear of Mexican "radicalism" as seen in the Constitution of 1917. The Red Scare of 1919 did nothing to help the situation. The Nation magazine, long an opponent of intervention in Mexico, bemoaned the general tenor of American newspapers, writing,

> If the Jingo press is to have its way, we are now clearly in sight of war with Mexico. Thus The New York Evening Sun cheerfully announces that "it is known to be the disposition of the Administration to stave off actual hostilities with Mexico to the last." Its headlines assert that "the country demands action in Mexico." than which nothing could be further from the truth. Having fought and won the war to end war, the country is sick of war, if not alas, of humbug. The Los Angles Times runs an anti-Mexico spread headline on its first page about every day, such as "Iron hand of American May Soon Be on Mexico," and "America May Rule Mexico. "...[I] n short, history is repeating itself; a Mexican war is being worked precisely as was the Spanish War, and the final argument is that it will be cheaper to do it now, and more humane, because we have an army of veterans all ready for the job. (The Nation 7/28/1919 p. 96)

By the end of 1919, there was widespread expectation that the United States would soon be at war with Mexico. Plans were being drawn up to deal with the logistical aspects of a war with Mexico. On November 22, 1919, the Washington Post carried a front page story titled "ARMY LAST RESORT IN MEXICAN CRISIS" The sub heading states that,

> General Staff Has Outlined Campaign Calling for Force of 450,000 Solider to Bring Order in Southern Republic and Estimates Three Years Occupation Would Be Necessary - Report

from Consular Agent Kidnapped by Bandits Reveals Indignities. (Washington Post 11/22/19 p. 1)

The reporter for the Washington Post, Albert W. Fox, opens his report by writing of the second arrest of Jenkins that,

> Although the second arrest of William 0. Jenkins, the American consular agent at Puebla is merely another indication of the approaching inevitable intervention by the United States in Mexico, it may serve to hasten the crisis in the relations between the two governments. (Fox Washington Post, 11/22/19 p. 1)

Two days later, the Washington Post carried another front-page article, entitled "READY FOR WAR IN AIR". This article started with the statement that

> "[W]ar in the air would play a big and spectacular part in the American invasion of Mexico, which may forced by the arrogant defiance of this government by Carranza." (Washington Post 11/24/19 p. 1)

People saw a government preparing for war, and the general tenor of the articles seems to indicate some broad-based support for such action. In addition to fears about Mexico, America was still under the influence of the Red Scare, fueled in large part by the actions of the Attorney General, A. Mitchell Palmer. The deportations of radical fit well with concerns over "bolshevism" in Mexico, as seen in the 'radical' Mexican Constitution of 1917.

The Outlook, a weekly magazine, wrote of the Jenkins case and what possible action Washington might take in its December 3 issue. The editors wrote,

As this issue of The Outlook goes to press Carranza's reply to the demand for the immediate release of Jenkins is hourly expected. A refusal of our demand ought to be met by vigorous action. Puebla is only some 135 miles as an airplane flies from Vera Cruz, and the dispatch of an American column for the release of the imprisoned Consular agent is not impracticable. (The Outlook The Jenkins Case 12/3/17 p. 390)

On December 4, 1919, the Washington Post reported an ominous turn of events that brought a union of Wilson's physical condition and the situation in Mexico. Fall was determined to force the issue, and was willing to use Wilson's stroke to political advantage. The headline on that day declared, "MEXICAN CRISIS, ACUTE, MAY RAISE QUESTION OF PRESIDENT'S DISABILITY"

On December 9, the same day that Wilson rejected Fall's suggestion that recognition of Carranza be withdrawn, the front page story in the Washington Post stated that "FALL UNMASKS MEXICAN PLOTS TO INCITE REVOLT AGAINST UNITED STATES-Carranza's Own Letters Prove Collusion Between Mexico's Rulers and Red Agitators Here." In the December 10 issue of The Outlook magazine, the editors wrote that of Mexico,

We can adopt the policy of intervention. There is a precedent for such a policy. In 1898 we took over Cuba, a Spanish-American country as Mexico is a Spanish-American country, established a protectorate over that island....We can do the same for Mexico. But task will be far more difficult and dangerous. We intervened in Cuba to free the Cubans from what we believed, and what many of them also believed, to be an intolerable foreign yoke. If we intervene in Mexico, it will be to save Mexicans from themselves. (The Outlook Mexico 12/10/19 p. 451)

In 1920 however, Mexico stated to back down. Carranza was now turning his efforts back to domestic politics. Barred by the 1917 constitution from running for President again, Carranza was seeking to install a candidate of his own choosing for the election of 1920. Carranza chose his Ambassador to the United States, Ignacio Bonillas. Carranza was starting to realize that for his faction to achieve effective control in Mexico, he would need to resolve some of the running disputes with United States.

Carranza was pragmatic enough to know that those who did not agree with him would not hesitate to use the gun rather than the ballot. Carranza had to adopt a policy that would satisfy the United States but not alienate his own domestic support.

During the Teapot Dome scandal of 1924 it was revealed that in 1917 Senator Fall and members of the oil industry had tried to devise a plan to partition the Northern states of Mexico. Their goal was to create a pro-United States "Oil Republic" (Meyers oil p. 70) That an invasion did not occur is a testament to the ideal that in the United States cooler heads, at times, prevail.

The impasse was finally resolved at the end of 1919 when the Mexican authorities started to issue provisional drilling permits. This was the last time that the Mexicans would try to enforce Article 27 until the Petroleum Law of 1925. This served as a somewhat anti-climatic resolution to the crisis.

Carranza turned towards supporting Bonillas while in the United States, the nation moved to elect its first post-War President. The American Presidential Election of 1920 was wide open. Wilson was in no shape, physically or politically, to run for reelection.

Given the failure of the Senate to ratify the treaty to join the League of Nations, did he have an inclination to run again either. The election was to be between the Republican Warren Harding and the Democrat James Cox. Harding's platform, was, in the simplest sense, a return to normalcy.

After the upheavals of the World War One and the Paris Peace Conference, Harding tapped into the current of American thought that sought quieter times and a favorable business climate. Foreign adventures held little appeal for most in the United States.

However, before the American election got into full swing, events in Mexico would alter the relationship between Mexico and the United State. Both Democrats and Republicans saw that a change in the Mexican government would allow a new administration to use recognition of a new Mexican administration as a tool to get Article 27 either scrapped or scaled back. Officials in both Mexico City and Washington knew that Obregon would not sit idly by while Carranza handed the election to Bonillas on a silver platter. Carranza made the opening move, ordering the arrest of Obregon and key supporters on March 30, 1920. The protests against Obregon's arrest were widespread, as Obregon enjoyed a large measure of popular support.

Concurrent at this time was a consolidation of power bases within Mexico. It would be the Sonorans who would wield power in Mexico during the 1920s. The numbers of players on the stage were also being reduced to eliminate political rivals. On April 10, 1920, Gonzalez's forces ambushed and killed Emilano Zapata in Morelos. The revolution was maturing from the phase of seeking power to consolidating power. With this consolidation, the more radical elements were being eliminated.

In Sonora, Obregon's home state, the Sonoran legislature declared its independence from the federal government in Mexico City, and all troops in Sonora were placed under the command of Plutarco Calles. Calles instigated a general revolt on April 15, 1920, and on April 22 issued their Plan de Agua Prieta. The plan denounced Carranza's violation of the Constitution and swore to,

> guarantee all legal protection and enforcement of their legal rights to citizens and foreigners, and…especially favour the development of industry, trade and all business (Bethell p. 194)

If the Sonoran revolt was not enough to keep Carranza occupied, Gonzalez, who had ordered the arrest of Jenkins the year before, unleashed a coup against Carranza on April 30. Carranza fled Mexico City on May 7, leaving the fight for power between the forces of Obregon and Gonzalez. In a sign of the growing stability (and maturity) in Mexican politics, Gonzalez and Obregon were able to reach some accommodation, rather than resorting to open combat for control of Mexico.

Gonzalez would allow a provisional presidential election, but would not disband his forces until after the election. On May 24, Adolfo De la Huerta was elected Provisional President. De la Huerta was a Sonoran, and had been elected Governor of Sonora in April, beating Carranza's candidate.

Carranza would never know of De la Huerta's election however, since he was killed on May 21 while trying to reach Vera Cruz to set up a "government in exile". Carranza's remaining forces faded into the background, and De la Huerta set September 5, 1920 as the date of the new election. With a government by coup however, Mexico was again without recognition from the United States. As an example of America's unchallenged position vis a vis Mexico, when the United States withdrew recognition, other nations followed suit. In the 1920's, the United States set the tone for the diplomatic status of nations in the Western hemisphere. Writes Camin and Meyers,

> None of the members of the international community could afford to ignore the indications from Washington on what should be done in the case of Mexico. England and Germany had disregarded Washington in the recent past without any result other than affecting their own interests. (Camin p. 80-81)

One of the issues facing the presidential candidates was under what conditions Mexico would regain recognition from the United States. As a sign of the changing, and increasingly pragmatic, view of Mexico, no one (aside from Woodrow Wilson) considered not recognizing the new government, only under what condition recognition would be granted.

That it came to power through a revolt was of increasing irrelevance to many in the United States. The only question in Washington was how much of the Mexican constitution could the United States suppress in exchange for recognition of the new regime. This reflected a view towards Mexico that in some ways ironically resembled the position taken by Taft in 1910. As long as the regime in power in Mexico was amiable to the interests of the United States, one could overlook the circumstances of its creation. Protection of investments had proven persuasive than moral positions.

Experience had taught that the imposition of a moral position or political system on another country was both difficult and tended to view with hostility. More importantly, the external imposition of a moral position was seldom successful. Many in Washington sought a more pragmatic approach, looking for a Mexican government that "they could work with."

Senator Fall suggested that any recognition of Mexico be tied to certain stipulations, among them a guarantee that American firms and citizens in Mexico be exempt from certain articles of the Constitution, especially Article 27. Fall also wanted to include a clause that if the Mexicans could not maintain order and stability, then the United States would do it for them. (Camin p. 81)

While De la Huerta wanted recognition from Washington, he could not, and would not, agree to such unreasonable terms. De la Huerta decided to leave the issue of American recognition to the next set of presidents, both in Mexico and the United States. With both countries spending the summer and fall of 1920 preparing for elections, foreign relations between the two were put on the back burner. Until a clear succession of power was made in both Mexico and the United States, little would be achieved on the diplomatic front.

With this position being adopted by De la Huerta, Mexico reverted to non-recognized status, and both Republicans and Democrats campaigned on what terms the re-recognition of Mexico would be cast. Dealing with issues now moved from the concrete to the abstract. Although no one knew it in the summer of 1920, relations with Mexico would be suspended until 1923.

The Republican candidate Harding won the election in the United States by a wide margin, beating Cox with 60% of the popular vote, and taking 404 electoral votes to win an easy victory. (Henretta p. A-16) The election of 1920 is also a milestone in American elections in that it was the first election since 1828 when less than 50% of eligible voters participated, with only 49.2% voting (Henretta p. A-16)

The 1920 campaign of the Republican Party spoke out against both Wilson's general foreign policy and his specific policy on Mexico. Wilson's policy towards Mexico over the previous eight years had done little to resolve the problems between Mexico and the United States. At times, such as Vera Cruz and the Jenkins affair, had proven to simply erode further the relationship between Washington and Mexico City, without a firm resolution of the problems between the two nations. The Republican Party platform stated that,

> The foreign policy of the Administration has been founded upon no principle and directed by no definite conception of our nation's rights and obligations. It has been humiliating to American and irritating to other nations, with the result that after a period of unexampled sacrifice, our motives are suspected, our moral influence impaired, and out Government stands discredited and friendless among the nations of the world. (Hart p.95)

The platform then directly attacks Wilson's policy towards Mexico, considering them ineffective and counterproductive. The general tone in the Republican Party was that Wilson had mishandled affairs in Mexico, and had done so to the detriment of America's prestige. If Wilson was going to use force, he should have used it to the full extent possible, with no holds barred. In part, the Republican Party platform called for a more consistent approach to Mexico, and to a policy that would reinforce America's prestige. The official part platform reads,

The ineffective policy of the present Administration in Mexican matters has been largely responsible for the continued loss of American lives in that country and upon our border; for the enormous loss of American and foreign property; for the lowering of American standards of morality and social relations with Mexicans, and for the brining of American ideals of justice, national honor and political integrity into contempt and ridicule in Mexico and throughout the world. (Hart p. 95)

> The Republicans did not object to Wilson's intervention in Mexico. Indeed, many in the party, such as Senator Fall, demanded greater action. Rather, the Republicans objected to the way in which Wilson had tried to mold events in Mexico with heavy-handed actions. The platform states,

The Republican party pledges itself to a consistent, firm and effective policy towards Mexico that shall enforce respect for the American flag and that shall protect the rights of American citizens lawfully in Mexico to security of life and enjoyment of property, in accordance with established principles of international law and our treaty rights. (Hart p. 96)

Harding was inaugurated as President on March 4, 1921. In his inaugural address, Harding made no mention of Mexico. Indeed, Mexico seemed to be fairly low on Harding's list of priorities. One indication of Harding's attitude was that Senator Fall was made the Secretary of the Interior. This gave the oil interests in the United States a voice to push their position before the President.

That voice would be a decidedly mixed blessing however, as Fall would be the first cabinet member to be convicted while in office. Fall was convicted for taking more than $ 300,000 in bribes to grant oil leases to industries. This corruption in Harding's administration would become known as the TeaPot Dome scandal.

With Harding in office, an offer was made to Obregon in May of 1921. The offer, in the form of a Treaty of Friendship and Trade, was a repackaging of the offer made by Fall in 1920. It demanded that the US be excluded from any enforcement of the Mexican Constitution, recognition of all oil rights held by Americans, and restitution for All-American property taken over since 1910.

Obregon could not accept such an offer, but he could not fully reject it. Obregon offered to negation a settlement if the United States would first grant him recognition. The United States rejected this proposal, and the impasse remained. What is important however, is that the two sides were talking with some regularity.

However, Obregon seemed to have learned something from the past years of conflict. Obregon left open the possibility of a resolution of the problem. In 1921, Obregon was able to convince the Mexican Supreme Court to agree that any legislation that would nationalize the oil industry would not apply to leases before 1917.

More importantly, Obregon dispatched De la Huerta, now the Minister of Finance to New York to work out a plan to repay Mexico's external debt, which had been in default for much of the past ten years. The debt level that Mexico owed was finally set at a level of $ 508,830,321. For the time, this was a staggering amount of money, considering that the total of American capital investment in the oil sector totaled a massive $ 500,000,000 in 1922.

The debt deal was important however, since it laid the foundation for more direct talks between the two sides. That Mexico was willing to work a debt-restructuring package proved that they were both serious about their financial obligations, and that the Mexicans may prove flexible in resolving the oil debate. To that end, both sides agreed to talks that were to be held in Mexico City. These talks would lead to what was known as the Bucareli Agreements of 1923.

CHAPTER TEN

▼

BUCARELI AGREEMENTS OF 1923

From May through August of 1923, the Mexicans and the Americans met in Mexico City to resolve the long-standing differences between the two sides. This meeting was not a high level diplomatic exchange, but rather a low-level discussion of issues.

The Bucareli Agreements served both the United States and Mexico. For the United States, Mexico agreed to set up compensation of North American losses in Mexico during the Revolution. In addition, Mexico stated that Article 27 would not be retroactive, based on the ruling in the Texas case. For Mexico, it was a chance to receive recognition once and for all.

The Mexican Supreme Court ruled that Article 27 would not be retroactive if positive acts had been taken. The concept of positive acts stated that if a company made improvements, such as drilling exploratory wells or other capital investment, than Article 27 would not be retroactive. This ruling gave the Mexicans some leeway as they felt they could apply Article 27 to lands that were being held in an unimproved state. With the interpretation of Article 27 finally settled, Mexico and the United States could get down to working out some accord to restore relations.

Obregon did not make these concessions out of a sense of goodness of his heart. The Bucareli Agreement was a pragmatic choice for Obregon and the future of Mexico. Obregon did so since he needed American support. In return for Mexican concessions, the United States agreed to grant recognition to Mexico. Obregon knew that when he left office in 1924, there would be a struggle for succession. He also knew that not everyone would accept his handpicked successor, Plutarco Calles.

In the fall of 1923, Pancho Villa was killed in a government led ambush, and so any threat from him was removed. Like the death of Zapata in 1919, the death of Villa represented a maturing of the Revolution and a consolidation of power by the surviving members of class of 1910. Villa and Zapata were eliminated, separately, since they both represented the most radical elements of the revolution. Mexico was entering the institutional phase of revolution, as the surviving members of the class of 1910 turned to building a nation.

In 1923, Aldopho de la Huerta launched a rebellion against Obregon. While bloody, it was short-lived since Obregon was able to turn to the United States for support. The United States quickly clamped down an arms embargo on de la Huerta's forces, and Obregon was able to crush the revolt.

The rebellion of de la Huerta was a great threat to Obregon, since over 60% of the army officers were in sympathy with rebel faction. (Bethell p. 206) The support of the United States was to play an essential role in putting down the coup attempt. Coolidge blockaded the Gulf so that the rebels could not obtain arms and so allow arms only to Obregon's forces.

Support and recognition from the United States was decisive, it that Washington took an active role in supporting Obregon's administration. After de la Huerta was put down, Plutarco Calles was elected President in 1924 before what Bethell writes was "the eyes of an indifferent nations."

(Bethell p. 207) The election of Calles also insured that Obregon had a chance to run for reelection in 1928.

Calles' relations with the United States were uneven, but would improve by 1928. In 1925, a new bondholder's agreement was achieved to separate railroad debt from all the other debt in the agreement of 1921. In December of 1925, Calles promoted a Petroleum Law and Alien Land Law bills. This law served as enabling legislation for Article 27, and caused a great deal of concern in the United States, since it ran counter to the understanding achieved in the Bucareli Agreement two years before.

The essential provision of this law was that the deeds to oil foreign own oil properties acquired before 1917 would be limited to 50 years. This was a direct violation of the Bucareli Agreements, and the United States protested strongly, but to no avail. In 1927, the Senate passed a resolution that called for continued arbitration of the situation, rather than intervention.

Another concern in 1925 was that Mexico was supporting Nicaraguan rebels (led by rebel leader Augusto C. Sandino) while the United States was supporting the Nicaraguan government. The United States would overcome Sandino's rebellion (but not Sandino himself, who would not lay down his arms until after the United States withdrew), and would occupy Nicaragua almost uninterrupted until 1933.

One source of tension in this period was internal to Mexico. In 1926, Calles facing criticism from the conservative, religious papers in Mexico sought to silence Church criticism once and for all. Under various amendments of the Mexican Constitution of 1917, (3,25,27 and 130) Calles sought to effectively ban the Catholic Church in Mexico. While the ability to do so had existed since 1917, no Mexican president had dared to challenge the Church, choosing instead to reach some accord with Church authorities.

On July 31, 1926, all religious services were banned in Mexico. While Calles had expected some resistance to his actions, he was not ready for what followed. Calles thought that be eliminating the Church, he would effectively silence criticism of his regime and eliminate fanaticism in Mexico.

When Church leaders objected, Calles replied that they had two avenues of recourse; "Congress or Arms" {Camin p. 86) When Congress rejected a petition signed by over 2 million Catholics, {Camin p. 86) the Church turned to the armed struggle.

Under the banner of Cristero Rey {Christ the King) a struggle ensued that was to last for three years. So widespread would be the fighting that the Army would be unable to put down the rebellion, and it would only be ended through negotiation, rather than a triumph of arms.

In the process, over 50,000 would be killed, and there would be great deal of concern of the suppression of the Catholic Church by Catholics in the United States. Many Catholics in the United States demanded intervention in Mexico to stop what they saw as the outright murder of Catholics in Mexico. As with other calls for intervention in Mexico, Coolidge opted for constructive engagement.

The rebellion ended in 1929 when both sides, with the help of the United States Ambassador, reached an agreement. Under this agreement, the Catholic authorities promised not to incite their followers to rebellion, and the government agreed not to interfere in Church affairs.

While there were tensions between Mexico and the United States in 1927, they paled in relations to problems in 1917. Both sides had matured in their positions, and more importantly, in how the dealt with one another. The greatest single example of this was the appointment of Dwight Morrow as the new Ambassador to Mexico.

One of the first successes of Morrow was that he got Calles to agree to make the petroleum law non-retroactive. With this concession, the greatest barrier between the United States and Mexico was removed. Morrow made small but important changes in how the United States dealt with Mexico.

One such change was the name on the United States Embassy in Mexico City. For years, the sign read "American Embassy" but Morrow changed it to "Embassy of the United States of America". A small change, but one which meant a great deal to the Mexicans. The United States acknowledged that they were not the only Americans.

EPILOGUE

---▼---

For all the promise of the Bucareli agreement in 1923, and Morrow's agreement with Calles, relations between Mexico and the United States would again falter in the 1930's, and would culminate with Mexico expropriation of foreign oil claims in Mexico.

In the end, the American struggle to influence Mexican controls over oil was a failure. Mexico won the battle by taking the one decisive step that Washington had spent 20 years trying to forestall nationalization. In 1937 oil workers struck in the oil fields, making demands of increased wages and better conditions.

The oil companies refused to comply, and both sides agreed to arbitration. The arbitration board made recommendation that added only slightly to the cost of the offer made by the oil companies, but the oil companies refused to go along. They took the case to the Mexican Supreme Court, and lost on appeal.

The oil companies ignored the ruling, and refused a final offer. In their arrogance, the oil companies felt that they were too important to the Mexican economy and that the workers and the Mexican government would give buckle. Mexico was now represented by Lazaro Cardenas as President, who was elected in 1934. Cardenas, now facing not only an economic crisis but also a matter of honor, did what many had talked about but few had considered; he expropriated the oil industry under the banner of a state oil company, Petrolos Mexicanos, better known as Pemex.

The response in Mexico was euphoria, for not in decades had the Mexican people been so united in a cause. Government bonds sold to cover claims against the appropriation were quickly snapped up like war bonds. Massive demonstrations were held to celebrate the breaking of the grip of foreign investors on Mexico's oil industry.

The celebration was not with problems, as American and British companies pulled investment money out of Mexico and started a boycott, refusing to sell spare parts and equipment to Pemex. Given this hurdle to development, the Mexicans still reveled in the fact that they now controlled Mexico's oil.

CONCLUSIONS

▼

Wilson in Retrospect

1919-1920 marked the end of Wilson's ability to influence events in Mexico as both the struggles for the Versailles Treaty and his stroke limited his effectiveness. The historical judgment on Wilson's policy would be that though well intentioned, it was in general a failure. Writes Lester Langly,

> For all his efforts, Woodrow Wilson was unable to manipulate the twentieth century's first modern revolution, nor did the persistent u.s. diplomatic pressures and military intrusions deter a generation of Mexican revolutionary leaders from defining that revolution. Warring among themselves over territory and influence, they united to produce a document -the 1917 Constitution- that was distinctively Mexican, a curious blend of nineteenth century liberalism in its exaltation of anticlericalism and of modern reformism in its affirmation of social justice...Wilson managed to keep the revolution within Mexican boundaries but, despite his benevolent professions and understanding, did little to shape its course. Yet he restrained more belligerent voices within his government who sought to crush the revolution, and his restraint

meant that the u.s.- Mexican relationship would take on a new, albeit uncertain, character. (Langley p. 17)

While seen as a failure, there is still a feeling that Wilson's shortcomings were not based on intent, but rather on how he sought to deal with Mexico. Jose Vasconcelos, Mexico's Minister of Education during this period, was a frequent critic of American policy. In 1928 however, in work for the Chicago Council on Foreign Relations, Vasconcelos takes a surprisingly sympathetic view Wilson, when one considers Vera Cruz and the Pershing expedition. Writes Vasconcelos,

As a rule, Mr. Wilson showed himself courteous and friendly. In all of his dealings with Mexico, perhaps as in all of the others acts of his public life, Mr. Wilson gave evidence of his honest and lofty temperament. His did not very often succeed and, what is worse, in many cases he did not use for a great purpose the enormous opportunities that fate had thrust upon his hand. Perhaps he was not bold enough to be a real idealist, but he was not mean enough to be merely practical. Taken as a whole, I believe, his stand toward Latin American ad Mexico will be remembered kindly among us, particularity when we compare it with the rash dollar- diplomacy which he persistently refused to serve. Had it not been for the unexplainable cases like the occupation of Santo Domingo and the Vera Cruz affair, Mr. Wilson could be classed as one of the founders of a true and hopeful Pan-Americanism. (Vasconcelos p. 134)

Wilson's policies towards Mexico have always required some sort of explanation of the duality of his approach. While Wilson supported the basic aims of the Revolution, such as self- determination, he was not hesitant to use force when things did not evolve in the way in did not like. At the same time however, Wilson was unwilling to yield to interventionist demands. Wilson goal was simple; getting the Mexicans to elect good men for their country.

Wilson also showed a somewhat dual approach in deciding whom he should support in Mexico. Wilson vacillated between supporting Villa and Carranza. In the end, he found that he could at least work with Carranza, if not always to his satisfaction. Write Haley,

> The problem, then, in dealing with Wilson's response to the Mexico Revolution is to explain both Wilson's intervention and his abstention, to explain what caused him to meddle constantly, with his unrealistic medication proposals, and what caused him to refuse to go to war against the Mexican Revolution and instead support the aims of the Mexican revolutionaries. The first part of the answer seems to lie in a paradox. The same beliefs that hampered Wilson's Mexican policy were also its greatest source of strength....Wilson tried to control developments in Mexico and force them into an American mold. But he avoided intervention against the Mexican Revolution because his belief in self- determination and social justice, founded on his understanding of the American Revolution and of contemporary American political and economic life, proved stronger than his missionary's desire to teach democracy to the world. (Haley p. 263)

While Wilson may deserve some criticism, he also deserves some praise. Although Wilson may have interfered in the internal affairs, others in the same position may have been driven to do much worse, such as a full invasion of Mexico. Wilson's failing, it seems in retrospect, is that he did little to try to understand the nature of the Mexican mind, and seemed to treat the laws of politics like the laws of physics; they would apply anywhere you used them, regardless of local conditions. He took what he saw as the American political model and tried to graft in onto the Mexican body politic without even bothering to translate it into Spanish. This was a method doomed to failure, as the American model was based on almost 150 years as a representative government. Mexico had no experience with democratic government, and had always been ruled by strong men. Elections in Mexico at this were not to see popular will, but legitimating choices already made by the power elite in Mexico.

With today's security advisors, country desks and CIA fact books, seems unreal that only 85 years ago a President would know so little about Mexico. His source of information, such as Hale and Lind, served him very poorly in his dealings with Mexico. His handling of the other great foreign policy crisis of his administration, the Great War, was handled with a much greater deftness.

But again, he failed in the end because he failed to fully understand the situation. Wilson's failure to take one major Republican with him to Versailles is an example of an arrogance that would effect his ability to effectively lead his nation. Wilson felt that he knew right from wrong, and that he needed no consensus take make decisions for the country.

While he could make decisions that have an impact on foreign policy, he needed the Senate in order to ratify that decision. This appears to be one of Wilson's failings. He acted as he saw fit, but took little notice of the political realities of building consensus.

Wilson did show a patience that others, such as Bull Moose candidate Theodore Roosevelt, would have not. It is not hard to imagine that a President Roosevelt elected in 1912 would have not hesitated to have used his powers to deal in a more forceful manner with Huerta. One can also see a President Roosevelt taking direct action against Mexico after the revelations of the Zimmerman telegram. Writes Parkes,

> Wilson's anxiety expressed itself in a series of moral lectures, interspersed with threats, on the beauties of peace and Constitutionalist and the right of foreigners in Mexico to protection-lectures that showed that Wilson, in spite of his friendliness, did not understand the differences between Mexico and the United States, and which

Mexicans found almost as irritating as the frank aggressiveness of dollar diplomacy. To these lectures Carranza replied by stubbornly refusing to make any concessions whatever. The United States, he declared, had no right to interfere, and foreigners in Mexico must expect to be treated no differently that natives. These assertions of national sovereignty counterbalanced, for many Mexicans, Carranza's deficiencies as a statesman; yet if anyone but Wilson had been President of the United States, the results might have been catastrophic. (Parkes p. 355-356)

However, the relationship between the United States and Mexico in this period also reflects other elements at work. Then, as today, every aspect of the relationship is colored by how the two sides perceive one another. The Mexican officials of 1917 had seen two US interventions into Mexico in the space of three years. Both interventions, Vera Cruz in 1914 and the Pershing Expedition of 1916 represented the violation of Mexico sovereignty.

American claims that they were protecting American interests falls flat when one considers that Vera Cruz, aside from being an excuse for getting rid of Huerta, was fought over a perceived slight by the American Naval Commander on the scene. It would be hard to picture the Commander of the U.S. Sixth Fleet shelling Cyprus because of the actions of an over zealous Cypriot military officer, or landing troops on Fiji due to a "disrespect" to the American flag.

Perhaps it is somewhat telling of Wilson personality (and perception) that he was shocked by the number of Mexican deaths at Vera Cruz, and he was surprised that the Mexicans would put up such a resistance to what he saw as a benign American action. If nothing else, Wilson seems to have repeatedly failed to come close to anticipating what actions his adversary would take.

American Policy 1910-1927

Relations between the United States and Mexico underwent a drastic change between 1917 and 1927. The change reflected in great part the attitudes of the major actors in this drama. Relations during the Wilson period were shaped as much by events (such as the Villa raid and the seizure of the crew of the U.S.S. Dolphin) as they were by long term policy goals on each side. At times the impending conflict between Wilson and Huerta were fueled by Wilson's personal beliefs in how a government should run as they were by the strategic threat (if any) that Huerta posed to the United States.

The main theme of this work sought to examine the threat of intervention. While there were always those agitating for action against Mexico, such as Senator Fall and Henry Lane Wilson, the United States, under both Democrats and Republicans, avoided direct military intervention in Mexico after 1917.

Perhaps one reason why successive administrations sought to avoid conflict with Mexico was that they had seen little gained from Vera Cruz and the Villa Expedition. The search for villa had uncovered nothing but Mexican hostility, and the invasion of Vera Cruz did nothing to build-up the relationship.

Once the pure threat of the safety of Americans was overcome the conflicts between the two sides moved to the problems in the relationship. After 1919, with a massive, well-trained Army that could be called to arms quickly, the only concerns Washington had with Mexico was the treatment of Americans and their investments in Mexico.

The relationship was effected by something as base as economics. Oil was an important resource, and the United States had invested heavily in its development. The United States could not, and would not, allow access to the oil to be cut off. In wartime the oil was needed to defeat the Central Powers; in peacetime it was needed to fuel the massive growth the United States experienced. America, on principle and economics, could not loose access.

That struggle, over oil and the implementation of Article 27, was to color the relationship between the two sides during this entire period. Some headway was made with the Bucareli Agreement in 1923. But even that success was short lived, as the two sides started squabbling over the details and interpretation. Given these disagreements, demand for intervention never reached the levels seen in 1917-1919. Whatever problems there were could be resolved without resorting to military force.

While this paper covers a period occupied by three Presidents, it is the influence and impact of the Wilson administration that casts the longest shadow. The major events of this paper: Vera Cruz, the Pershing Expedition and the Constitution of 1917 all occurred during Wilson's tenure.

In addition, Wilson made Mexico an area of his concern, ironic in part since Wilson entered the White House with little desire to major foreign policy a major part of his administration. Mexico could have been another diplomatic backwater had Wilson not made it a major issue.

In sharp contrast, the approach of the Harding and Coolidge Administrations sought to resolve points of conflict through bilateral discussion. This conflict also shows the differences in emphasis between Wilson and his successors. At times, Wilson seems almost preoccupied with Mexico, as he appears unable to put his academic theories of proper government into practice.

It would be under Harding and Coolidge that a more pragmatic approach to the Mexican issue would be found. When the Revolutionary powers in Mexico showed that they were willing to make deals, Coolidge sought to work with the Mexicans.

Whatever conflicts existed, Coolidge was willing to try and reach some accommodation. While there were major flaws in the some of the agreements, it was better than fighting a war with Mexico. The signing of Bucareli Agreements is a testament to the wisdom of this approach. As flawed as the agreements may have been, the represented a willingness to invest the time and effort to resolve the pending issues with Mexico through diplomatic means. While the end result in 1938 was expropriation, that does not mean that American policy in this period was doomed to fail. The Great Depression of the 1930's had a great impact on the ability of Mexico to pay her debts or sell her oil for export. In 1927, relations were moving towards a new era were Mexico was treated more like an equal and less like an unruly schoolboy.

About the Author

▼

Drew Philip Halévy received a BA in Political Science from UNC-Greensboro in 1988 and an MA in Government in 1991. He has also attended the University of Arkansas, where he received Secondary Education certification in Social Studies. From 1994-1996, he was in the PhD program in the history department.

REFERENCES

▼

Atkins, Ronald Revolution! Mexico 1910-1920 London: Macmillan, 1969

Bailey, David C !Viva Cristo Rey! The Cristero Rebellion and the Church-State Conflict in Mexico by David C. Bailey. Austin, University of Texas Press 1974

Bemis, Samuel Flagg A diplomatic history of the United States. New York, Holt 1950

Bethell, Leslie Mexico Since Independence New York: Cambridge University Press, 1991

Callahan, James Morton American Foreign Policy in Mexican Relations New York: Macmillan, 1932

Camin, Hector & Meyer, Lorenzo In the Shadow of the Mexican Revolution Austin, TX: University of Texas Press, 1993

Cockcroft, James D. Latin American History, Politics and US Policy Chicago: Nelson-Hall Publishers, 1996

Creel, George The People Next Door New York: The John Day Company, 1926

Crow, John Armstrong The epic of Latin America Los Angles. university of California Press., 1992

Eisenhower, John S. D., Intervention! : The United States and the Mexican Revolution New York: w.w. Norton, 1993

Ellis, Ethan Frank B. Kellogg and American Foreign Relations 1925-1929 New Brunswick, NJ: Rutgers University Press, 1961

Gilderhus, Mark T. Diplomacy and revolution: U.S.-Mexican relations under Wilson and Carranza era Tucson: University of Arizona Press, 1977

Haley, P. Edward Revolution and Intervention The Diplomacy of Taft and Wilson with Mexico, 1910-1917 Cambridge, MA: MIT Press, 1970

Hall, Linda Revolution of the Border the United States and Mexico, 1910-1920 Albuquerque, NM: University of New Mexico Press, 1986

Hart, George L. Official Report of the Proceedings of the Eighteenth Republican National Convention New York: Tenny Press, 1924

Hart, George L. Official Report of the Proceedings of the Seventeenth Republican National Convention New York: Tenny Press, 1920

Henretta, James A. et al America's History New York: Worth Publishers, 1993

Knight, Alan The Mexican Revolution New York: Cambridge University Press, 1986

Langley, Lester D. America and the Americas: the United States in the Western Hemisphere Athens, GA: University of Georgia Press, 1989

Lowenthal, Abraham F. Partners in conflict, the United States and Latin America Baltimore, Md.: Johns Hopkins University Press, 1987 Matloff, Maurice (ed.) American Military History Volume 21902-1996 Conshohoken, PA: Combined Books, 1996

Meyer, Lorenzo (trans. by Muriel Vasconcellos) Mexico and the United States in the oil Controversy, 1917-1942 Austin, TX: University of Texas Press, 1977

Needler, Martin C. Latin American politics in perspective Princeton, N.J., Van Nostrand, 1967

Parkes, Henry Bamford A History of Mexico Boston: Houghton Mifflin Company, 1969

Pastor, Robert A Castaneda, Jorge. Limits to friendship: the United States and Mexico New York: Knopf, 1988

Paz, Octivao The Labyrinth of Solitude New York: Grove Press, 1961

Quirk, Robert E An affair of honor; Woodrow Wilson and the occupation of Vera Cruz Lexington, KY: University of Kentucky Press, 1962

Richmond, Douglas W. Essays on the Mexican War Grand Prairie, TX: Texas A & M University Press, 1986

Riding, Alan Distant Neighbors A Portrait of the Mexicans New York: Vintage Books, 1986

Rippy J. Fred, Vasconcelos, Jose and Stevens, Guy Mexico Chicago, Ill: The University of Chicago Press, 1928

Rodman, Selden, A short history of Mexico New York: Stein and Day, 1982

Ruiz, Ramon Eduardo The Great Rebellion New York: WW Norton & Company, 1980

Schmitt, Karl M. Mexico and the United States 1821-1973 Conflict and Coexistence New York: John Wiley and Sons, 1974

Simpson, Lesley Byrd Many Mexico's Berkley: University of California Press, 1971

Tannenbaum, Frank Ten Keys to Latin America New York: Vintage Books, 1962

Tuchman, Barbara The Zimmermann Telegram New York: Viking Press, 1958

US Government Printing Office Foreign Relations of the United States: The Lansing Papers Washington, D.C.: US Government Printing Office, 1940

US Government Printing Office Foreign Relations of the United States 1917 Washington, D.C.: US Government Printing Office, 1924

US Government Printing Office Foreign Relations of the United States 1918 Washington, D.C.: US Government Printing Office, 1925

Wilson, Woodrow The Papers of Woodrow Wilson vol. 64 Princeton, NJ: Princeton University Press, 1983

www.ingramcontent.com/pod-product-compliance
Lightning Source LLC
Chambersburg PA
CBHW020303290526
45784CB00003B/1349